FINDING TRUE LOVE THROUGH ONLINE DATING

FINDING TRUE LOVE THROUGH ONLINE DATING

A Christian Woman's Guide

MARICEL COLQUIT

Really Good Content LLC

Introduction

"Can you really find true love online?" This is one of the most common questions I often get asked. My short and simple answer is an unequivocal yes. Because that's exactly what happened to me, and I can't think of a logical explanation why it can't happen to you. The next question that often follows this is, "How?" And that's precisely why I wrote this book, to show you how you, too, can find your own true love online.

In this book, I reveal the secrets to crafting an irresistible online dating profile—what to write and what not to write. What to look for in a profile and what your potential mate will be looking for in your own profile. I recommend the top three dating sites that I personally used. I outline the advantages and disadvantages of online dating as well as safety tips that you should follow. I provide an exhaustive list of questions that can help you break the ice and get to know a prospective partner in life better. I address commonly asked online dating questions that might be plaguing you, and so much more.

I know exactly where you might be right now. I, too, waited, fasted, and prayed for my future husband all my life.

I remained faithful and preserved myself for 40 years. There were times I thought I'd never get married. But then, in the most unexpected way, God answered my prayers through an online dating site. God gave me an amazing man who turned out to be everything I have prayed for, and even more than I could have ever hoped for. We have been happily married since. That's why I am excited to share with you my own experiences, good and bad, so you can learn and benefit from them. So you can avoid the mistakes I made.

The struggle is real; I know. But you do not have to go through life alone anymore. You do not have to wait any longer either. Give online dating a try. It may just be the right channel for you. Millions have already met their spouses online. It's time for you to have the same success. While I cannot guarantee that you will find your own true love online, I can promise that this book will increase your chances of finding the godly man (or woman) of your dreams.

But do not delay. If you do not act now, you could end up waiting all your life. The tips and tricks you're about to read will surely help you navigate the complex online dating world like a pro. Each chapter walks you through everything you need to know so you can have an exciting and positive experience. If you follow my advice in this book, there's no reason why you won't find your own true love online.

Contents

To my amazing husband, Cantrell Colquit. Thank you for finding me and loving me the way you do. You are more than I could have ever hoped for.

ISBN: 979-8-9878382-1-1 (Paperback)
ISBN: 979-8-9878382-0-4 (Ebook)

Book Cover by Kumuditha Herath

Really Good Content LLC

www.maricelcolquit.com

I

40 And Waiting

"Why, God, why? Why is it so hard to find a true, godly man? Will I ever find true love? Are there really no good men left out there?"

The 40-year-old woman cried out to God, banging her hands against the wheel of her white Toyota Matrix as she cruised down I-4 in Orlando. The woman had just ditched a date in Tarpon Springs, a city in Florida off the coast of the Gulf of Mexico. This was her second date with the man she first met online. She thought she had finally found a genuine Christian guy. He ticked all the boxes. He was single, had never been married, was good-looking, active at church, and knew the Bible well. So where did she fail? How did she miss the signs? The lady had just found out an hour earlier that the man she was dating was a fraud. She felt duped and deflated.

Never again, she thought. Never again would she make the same mistake, she promised herself.

That 40-year-old woman was me five years ago. You see, I was in the exact same spot as you probably are: single, frustrated, feeling alone, forgotten, and neglected by God, waiting for your future spouse for what seemed like forever. Like you, I have waited for my husband all my life. I tossed and turned in bed for what seemed like an eternity, often with tears streaming down my face relentlessly. I can remember asking God a thousand times, "How long, O Lord, how long?" The wait was painfully palpable, intensified by the fact that I was in a foreign land, thousands of miles away from my homeland.

As you must have imagined, I wasn't always like this. I didn't find myself longing deeply for my future husband until I was in my late 20s. As a high schooler, I always thought I would be married and settled at 25. But shortly before I turned 25, I realized there was so much more for me to see and do. I wanted to explore the world. Getting married would ruin all that—at least that's what I thought. So, at 26, I packed my bags, left my country, and moved to Dubai, a melting pot of cultures. Nothing could have been more fitting than Dubai as the best launching pad to explore the world. Little did I know that my excitement would gradually be snuffed out by the city's glitz and glamour.

One and a half years after arriving in Dubai, with the world as my oyster, I started exploring the United Arab Emirates' contiguous countries. Israel was at the top of my list, as it had been my lifelong dream to see it. Living in Dubai at the time meant I could not travel directly to Israel without risking my UAE visa. Flying into Jordan was the next best option, so that's exactly what I did. After an arduous bus ride, I got dropped off at the wrong hotel in Petra, world-renowned for its Nabatean ruins in the southwestern part of Jordan. The manager of the wrong hotel graciously offered to take me to the right hotel and show me the city later. Not knowing anyone in the small city, which looked more like a small village to me, I was more than happy to accept.

Deep inside, curiosity had gotten the best of me. I didn't know it then, but loneliness had crept in. The hours-long public bus ride to Petra left me questioning what I was doing with my life. There I was, a 28-year-old, traveling solo through the rugged mountains of Jordan. I had purposefully preserved myself my entire life and refused to date casually. I started questioning whether all the waiting or preserving was even worth it. I had not even been kissed. I longed for my future boyfriend's embrace. I had not gone out on an official date either, as I wanted my first boyfriend to be my first date. Yes, I had admirers. I had pursuers. I also had male friends I hung out with, but I didn't see any of our get-togethers as real dates.

I wondered what it would be like to go out with somebody officially. The deeper I got into the heart of the Jordanian wilderness, the lonelier I got, and the stronger the urge to take the risk was. Nobody knew me in Petra, so what did I have to lose? I sensed that I shouldn't go but ignored my gut feeling. I wanted to break my self-imposed rules for once. So I said yes to the stranger. Sure enough, just before dark, the hotel manager picked me up and told me he was going to take me to a place called Little Petra. He bragged about its most beautiful starry sky ever, which only got me excited. Unbeknownst to me, Little Petra was in the middle of the village but isolated enough that none of the villagers could see or hear us.

By then, it was too late for me to leave or escape. Darkness had enveloped the entire area. Acting blasé, I pretended I was totally comfortable in my surroundings while praying fervently and silently. The last thing I wanted was for the man to sense my fear. Granted, the man looked harmless enough. He was a little bony and only about 5'6 tall—not menacing or overpowering. However, I was keenly aware of the precarious situation I was in. The man pointed upward. I looked up and saw that the night sky was a blanket of stars, with the Milky Way almost crystal clear. The stars looked so big and so near, as if they were within our reach. The whole skyscape took my breath away. It sure was the most glorious and starry sky I had ever seen in my life.

After about an hour of stargazing and polite comments, we made our way back into town. Although the night sky was so breathtaking, I was more than happy to get out of Little Petra in one piece. I thanked the man profusely and said goodbye. To be fair, he was a perfect gentleman the entire time. He didn't even try to touch my hand, but still. You would think I would have learned my lesson, but no. After exploring Petra for a few more days, I joined other hotel guests in exploring Wadi Rum. We then made our way to Aqaba, a coastal city in Jordan. In Aqaba, I bumped into an Italian Jordanian man who claimed to be a master scuba diver. He offered to take me snorkeling.

Since I had heard so much about how beautiful the Red Sea was, I thought the opportunity was too incredible to pass up. I had quickly forgotten about my daring exploit with the stranger in Petra. I was a relatively good swimmer at the time. We'd stay on the shore, so how dangerous could it get? Again, I ignored the warning signs not to go. I felt like a bird that had been set free from its cage, so I said yes again. If anything, since nothing happened to me in Little Petra, it may have emboldened me to try again. The man had a driver who took us to a less crowded part of the beach along the Red Sea. First red flag.

I was really hoping we would be among the crowd. I quickly knew the man was up to no good. Once again, I felt trapped. I ran to the sea excitedly, trying to make light of the situation. At first, the Jordanian pretended to be a gentleman. He patiently guided me and showed me the bright and colorful world under the sea. He pointed out the different kinds of fish and corrals underneath. He may have been telling the truth about being a master scuba diver after all. Before we knew it, the sun was already setting. The man grabbed me from the back and held me in his arms in the water. "So, this is it," I thought. "First, a hug, then maybe a kiss. Then, what? Is this what happens on a 'real' date?"

I quickly regretted my decision to come. What was I thinking? I didn't want the stranger to be my first kiss. But what could I do if he forced me? And what if he doesn't stop there? Again, all I could do was pray silently and desperately that God would somehow rescue me for the second time in a row. I was well aware that I had put myself in a similar situation once again. I begged God to spare me just the same. I promised that I would never give in to my loneliness and curiosity again. By then, the beach was almost empty. Fear crept up my spine. Even if I screamed, I didn't think anybody would come to my rescue. Being in a Middle Eastern country, some might even blame me instead.

But God proved Himself faithful once again despite my unfaithfulness. After brushing off more advances from him, the man abruptly gave up and asked the driver to take me back to my hotel. I was floored. I could not believe he was letting me go just like that. I held my breath until I reached my hotel safely. Looking back, my dangerous escapades made me realize how my loneliness made me so vulnerable. 1 Peter 5:8 clearly warns us to be watchful as the devil prowls like a roaring lion, seeking someone to devour. I could have easily been devoured if not for God's grace.

It made me realize that it's true that one can never play with fire without getting burned. This is surely the reason why so many Christians often fall. They willingly put themselves in a compromising situation, thinking they could handle it and resist the temptation. But far too many regret their decisions more than those who escape unscathed, as I did. Unfortunately, Satan knows our weaknesses better than we do. He attacks us at the most opportune moment, when we least expect it. I never imagined that after waiting for 28 years, I would give in just like that. True, I was just curious about dating. I just wanted to experience it. But I didn't want the physical aspect of it. I just wanted to enjoy spending time with someone.

But what could I possibly expect from an ungodly man? I realized going on an official date is not all it's cracked up to be. On the other hand, it also made me wonder about my future husband. It made me wonder if all my waiting and preserving had been worth it after all. Twice, I put myself in a dangerous situation. Twice, I was rescued. Surely, God must have somebody out there for me? Surely, he must be somebody truly special? Why did God save and preserve me, then? My trips taught me a valuable lesson, but they also fueled a deeper hunger to see more of the world. Dating took the back seat while church, work, and occasional travel took the front seats. Sure, I was still curious about dating and relationships, but they were never a priority.

I wished I could have stopped the time, but I couldn't. The dreaded 40 came in the blink of an eye. By then, I was resigned to the fact that I may never get married. Around the same time, I sensed God was taking me to the USA. Although I wanted to go to the U.S. for a visit, I did not want to live there. But as always, I surrendered my will and obeyed God. So, at 40, by faith, I left the vibrant city of Dubai for good and landed in New York. I only had three suitcases and a meager $10,000 to start a new life in America. I had also accepted a missionary post at a nonprofit in Orlando as assistant director of marketing. I did not know what the future held, but I was confident I was where God wanted me to be. It was all up to Him to make things happen.

My job was to trust in Divine Providence and wait for His plans to unravel in His time and way. Matthew 6:25–34 had taken on a whole new meaning to me. I tried hard not to worry, but it wasn't always easy. On top of my financial worries, I also had to deal with the emotional challenges of not having anyone to lean on. But I didn't know if marriage was even in the cards for me. And that's how, at 40, I found myself crying on I-4 in Orlando, where I started this chapter.

I was 40 and waiting for my husband-to-be, with no money and no honey. I was frustrated, dejected, and alone, with no prospects in sight. The future didn't look so bright either. Or so I thought.

I'm sure many of you can relate to some or all of my struggles and challenges. Perhaps, like me, you have preserved yourself all your life but with no prospects either. I once met a 50-year-old woman who had been waiting for her future spouse. Her question was, "What about me? I have served God faithfully, but why am I still single?" I knew exactly how she felt because I was in the same boat as she was. All I could tell her was that I did not know God's plans for her. But I did know that God had a plan and would reveal it to her in His own time. I encouraged her to keep the faith because God surely knew what she was going through.

I have met other women in their 50s who are still waiting for their spouses. Some were faithfully waiting while some were frustrated with the seemingly endless wait. I have also personally met much younger Christian women who simply gave up and married ungodly men because they could not wait any longer. None of them were happy with their decisions. I have also met other women who preserved themselves but got impatient and gave in. They weren't proud of their decisions either, and deeply regretted their actions. If you are in any one of these situations, take courage. We serve a gracious God who is able to wash you, help you, and redeem you. Just call on Him and surrender your life to Jesus once more.

1 John 1:9 exhorts us: "If we confess our sins, he is faithful and just to forgive us our sins and to cleanse us from all un-righteousness." There is no reason for you to feel condemned.

You are forgiven; you are free. Some of you might also be asking, "Well, if your God was really good, why did He make you wait so long?" That's okay; I myself have asked that same question. Well, almost a similar question. I never questioned God's goodness, but I did wonder why many times. It took quite a while before I finally found the answer. I believe God allowed me to wait for so long so that one day I can share my story with you and, hopefully, with other people around the world.

Even after accepting my role at the nonprofit in Orlando, I always believed that there was something bigger or greater that God had planned for me in the U.S. And I believe it is this—that I share my own story of waiting and overcoming through this book so others, including you, may be uplifted. God is no respecter of persons; that is, He does not play favorites. Just as God has done it for me, He will do it for you too. Just as I have waited, you can too. Just as I triumphed, you can too. Just as I walked the lonely path of singleness and overcame it, so can you. To let you know that, in the end, the reward far outweighs the pain.

2

Stuck With "The One"

"There is someone created just for you."

I'm sure you've heard this before, perhaps directly from the pulpit, or through a third party. The internet is rife with articles on this, and hundreds of books propagate the same. I've met people who completely embraced this, even though they were already in their third or fourth marriage. It always baffled me. How many "the ones" can a person possibly have? Their situation alone suggested the exact opposite of what they believed. How can one possibly marry so many "The Ones?" That's a complete oxymoron. Could this be the reason why so many Christians get married so fast and divorce soon after when they believe they married the wrong person?

This practice or belief is not only flawed but also antithetical to what the Bible says. But the bigger question is, "Is there really such a thing as 'The One'?" Before I get into the nitty-gritty details of online dating, I feel compelled to address this controversial teaching, mainly because I spent my early days as a new Christian believing and embracing this same doctrine myself. I not only believed it, I lived it. I came to really know the Lord Jesus Christ through a student fellowship in my university. The group was big enough to be considered a church. We did street evangelism and had prayer meetings every weekday at 5:30 a.m. on the right side of the campus library.

Although I was already a professing Christian when I first joined the group, I realized there was so much I could learn from the members. They were all so polite, behaved, loving, and caring. They always talked about God and thanked Him before they ate their food. They were so different from the people that I knew back at my church in the province. In my old church, people seemed to talk the talk but not walk the walk. In huge contrast, members of my university group were devoted to the Word and passionate about holiness. It was one thing to hear people talk about the Bible, but it was another thing to actually see others live it.

I felt like I had found a heavenly fellowship. As I got to know the leaders of the group, I started learning more about the group's beginnings. I realized that the senior pastor was the founder of the group and was led to the Lord by his friend. Whether the senior pastor had somebody overseeing him, I didn't know. He seemed highly intelligent and articulate. I was like a sponge. I absorbed everything he said and hung on his every word. Although every leader or pastor encouraged us to double-check what they preached against the Bible, I did not.

The leaders all sounded like they knew what they were talking about. They mostly resonated with what I already knew to boot. I did read the Bible personally, but mostly for my own satisfaction and spiritual nourishment. Not necessarily to verify that what they were preaching to us was accurate and/or biblically aligned. So, during one of our Bible studies, when one of the pastors stated that there was one person created just for us, I believed him without question. I thought it made sense. God created Eve for Adam. Surely, there must be an Adam created just for me? Right.

I graduated four years later, fully convinced that I did not have to search for or look for my "The One." It was my Adam's job to look for me. No matter where I was in the world, God would surely bring us together. He would know it was me who was meant for him, and I would know he was the one meant for me instantly. There would be no question. Our leaders clearly lived this out by encouraging us to marry within the group. Even our senior pastor married one of the female members he used to disciple. There was nothing wrong with that at all. But prior to this, he was engaged to someone else who was also a member of the group. People wondered how "The One" applied in this scenario. Did the pastor make a mistake and got engaged to the wrong "The One" previously?

What will happen to the former fiancée? Will she find a different "The One"? But how does that work? Will the one she finds next be "second best" since she's been engaged before? And what about us? Will we make the same mistake too? It was confusing and almost convoluted, but I tried to brush it off since it wasn't my business. But maybe I should have made it my business to ensure that I understood the doctrine correctly. But I didn't. I continued actively participating in the group. But deep inside, I had some lingering doubts about what we were doing. Were we doing things right, or were we going to extremes? Were we misinterpreting the Bible somehow? But I never once voiced my concerns. In retrospect, maybe I should have.

Not that I am trying to malign the group or the leaders. I truly appreciated being a part of that group. I always attribute my strong Christian roots to them. They taught me so much. The pros outweighed the cons. But the doctrine of "The One" was deeply ingrained in my brain. Even after leaving campus and graduating from college, I lived my life waiting for "The One" until I moved to Dubai. With very limited churches to choose from, I joined an evangelical church. I was readily impressed with how good they were at unpacking the Word.

During one of the church's weekly Bible classes, the facilitator touched on the concept of "The One." He said that it wasn't true or that it didn't exist. That only after we marry the person will we know if he or she was "The One." My brain almost exploded. I wanted to run out of the room. But something in me told me to stay and listen. Could he possibly be right? The more I listened, the more I thought it made more sense. Later that night, I grabbed my Bible and dug deeper into it. That was when I was led back to the text in 1 Corinthians 7:39: "The wife is bound by the law as long as her husband liveth; but if her husband be dead, she is at liberty to be married to whom she will; only in the Lord."

I had read that verse so many times before, but it never really spoke to me. Suddenly, the words seemed to be jumping up at me. The text clearly said, "she is free to marry anyone she wishes." The key word was "anyone." How can there be "The One" when we can clearly marry anyone? And not just anyone, but anyone we wish. So, it was not even up to God. It was actually up to us to decide who to marry. The only stipulation was "only in the Lord." Meaning, whoever we choose to marry must be a believer. He cannot be an unbeliever, hands down. There was no misinterpreting this verse or the rest of the chapter.

My jaw dropped. It was a shocker, but it was also an eye-opener. I could not believe I had missed it all these years. I thought of all the wasted time. And what about those godly men I pushed away because I thought none of them was "The One" for me? Was it possible that God brought me a potential mate in the past, but I let him get away because I was holding on to a false belief? My heart sank. I was crushed and thankful at the same time. I could not believe I had embraced an unbiblical doctrine all my Christian life. I remembered the things I said and did to get rid of the godly men who came my way. How could I? I was driven by fear of falling for the wrong "One," but that was no excuse. I repented and asked God for forgiveness.

I honestly thought I was doing the men a favor. I feared I was taking them away from someone they were meant to be with. But it was also quite freeing to know that I was no longer bound by a false doctrine. I knew it was time to turn a new leaf—to have a fresh start and a clean slate. A few years later, I met somebody who had been married three times but was still believing in "The One." I realized how pervasive this teaching was in churches across the world. That's why I was convicted to address this contentious teaching before continuing. It is no wonder that so many single women still shun online dating.

Many of them believed that if they tried online dating, they would be helping God the way Sarah helped God by having her own baby through Hagar. Some believe that they should just wait for "The One" to show up on their doorstep, just like I used to believe. True, it does happen sometimes, but rarely. God does miraculously speak to men and women of God and let them know that the person in front of them is the right person for them. But if we were not in tune with God, how could we possibly hear Him? If we were not sensitive to the leading of the Holy Spirit, how could we possibly know? Sadly, so many women end up waiting endlessly for something that might never happen. All because of a misaligned doctrine.

If you have embraced this doctrine yourself, I hope you also find it liberating to know. And if you have wasted years of your life believing in it, please don't be hard on yourself. As I mentioned, I've also been there and done that. It's never too late to repent and start over. Just surrender everything to God. It wasn't your fault. I don't blame my former leaders, either. They inadvertently misinterpreted the Bible. I can only wish that I had done my research sooner. Or that I questioned the doctrine sooner. My prayer is that any other pastor or church leader still preaching this wrong doctrine will change course and retract. No one will blame them for unintentionally misleading their members.

On the other hand, I would be even more remiss if I didn't talk about the real "The One." I know I just told you that "The One" does not exist. Well, this one is different; out of this world, in fact. This one was sent to earth to show you how precious you are. This was The One who paid the ultimate price for you so you might live. The One who gave up everything so you may have everything you need. The One who can fulfill and satisfy you like no one else can. The One who loves you more than any man ever can and more than you will ever know. I really hope that you will meet The One in the pages of this book, for He is truly worth your time. He is infallible and incomparable to no one. And not just meet, but fall deeply in love with "The One."

3

Is Online Dating for You?

"I don't think online dating is for me."

"Online dating is for desperate people!"

"There is no way I'm going to try online dating. I'm not that desperate."

"Why on earth would I try online dating!?"

You have probably heard these scathing comments before. They either made you cringe or made you laugh. Or maybe these comments made you cry as they cut like a knife. Perhaps you're someone who decided not to try online dating because you didn't want to be labeled desperate. Or maybe you've already tried online dating, but you're hiding the fact for obvious reasons. You dare not let people know that you are actually contemplating online dating, either. And if you're actively dating someone you met online, you're probably doing it like a cloak-and-dagger operation. Or maybe, just maybe, you married somebody you met online, like I did, and you don't want people to know how you met.

I know. I get it. To be honest, I used to feel embarrassed about it too. I used to not want people to know that my husband and I met online. Apparently, I'm not the only one. According to an article on Today, this is more common than we think. (Patteson, 2020) I shuddered at the thought of earning people's ire. Or their judgment, heaven forbid. Even today, the stigma still exists among church leaders. (Coates, 2013)

But then, later on, I realized there really was no reason for me to be mortified. Why should I? God gave me such a wonderful husband through online dating, so why should it matter? Is the "how" or "where" more important than the "who"? Unfortunately, my concerns were not baseless. A couple from my old church in Dubai, where I used to live, once accused me of being desperate simply for creating an online profile. They called me out for allegedly prioritizing online dating over God. Phew. I will talk more about our encounter in a subsequent chapter.

I know these comments may seem earth-shattering at first, but trust me, you will eventually get over them. You will learn to brush them off. At the end of the day, who really cares about other people's opinions? Only God's opinion of us matters. It's your love life, not others', that's at stake. So, keep doing what you're doing and keep your head high. I know several people who met their spouses in person but are in miserable marriages right now. It's almost common nowadays to meet someone at church who is in their third or fourth marriage. These are people who met their partners in person. I have yet to hear of couples who met online and are facing divorce. So, what gives? That's why I finally told myself that I should stop hiding the fact that I met my husband online.

What matters is that my husband and I are happily married and plan to stay married for the rest of our lives. It just makes no sense that people tend to give emphasis on such trivial matters. Our society seemingly has its relationship priorities completely backwards. It's no wonder that the U.S. has the third highest divorce rate globally, according to an article by Legaljobs. (Vuleta, 2022) I also find it laughable that most of those who scoff at online dating are the ones who actually struggle to find somebody in person. I know women who are as closed-minded as this. I wouldn't be surprised if those women remained single for the rest of their lives.

But the fact that you are reading this means you are actually open-minded. You have contemplated trying online dating, but you're wondering if it's really for you or not. You do not believe that online dating is for desperate people either. You actually see online dating as a tool for God to bring potential mates together. You have also probably wondered if the online dating success stories you've heard were true. Is it really possible to find true love online? You've asked yourself if that could happen to you, too. You want to try online dating but don't know where to start. You're vacillating because you've also heard horrible stories. What if it happens to you too? Your mind must be flooded with questions, doubts, and concerns.

How do you know if it is safe? How do you know if the bad things that happened to others will not happen to you?

What if you fall in love with someone who is not who he (or she) claims to be? You have so many unanswered questions, and you do not know who to ask or where to find the answer. And that's where I come in, or where this book comes in. I wanted to assure you that online dating is not as bad as some people would have you believe. As exemplified by some, online dating is not for everyone either. There are many skeptics out there. You just have to accept that. But what they say or do is irrelevant. In the end, there are far more believers out there than skeptics. Focus on those who inspire you, and forget about the few naysayers.

However, just because online dating isn't for some doesn't mean it isn't for you. Just because some people think you are desperate doesn't mean you are. So what if people talk about you? You can't stop them from talking anyway. Just see them as ducks that like to quack. Remember the difference between ducks and eagles? Ducks quack while eagles soar above the clouds. Up there in the clouds is probably where you'll meet your fellow eagle (future spouse). Who knows? Maybe he (or she) has been waiting there for you all this time. Just focus on what you really desire—a life partner. Walk through whatever door God opens up for you, whether online or offline. Besides, you will probably meet more men (or women) online than you ever will in real life. Not to mention that online dating is quite beneficial if you are socially awkward.

As I mentioned in my introduction (please go back if you haven't read it yet), I never expected to meet my husband online. In fact, I was one of those people who believed that online dating was for desperate people. Even my husband thought the same for years. Long before my husband and I met online, we both met couples who met online and got married. Although we were happy for our respective friends, we both quietly thought that we were not going to try online dating ourselves. But look how far we have fallen. We must have been desperate then?

Joking aside, even while I was still in college, I always wanted to go to Israel. I longed to live and work there. But to be honest, I was dreaming that I would meet a good Messianic Jew that I could marry. A few years later, God was gracious enough to fulfill my dreams of going to Israel, but only as a tourist. But the only jobs available for Filipinos then were non-professional jobs, so I did not even try. I had no inclinations either, as I wanted to travel and explore, something I was able to do with my job in Dubai at the time. And clearly, I did not meet anyone suitable in Jerusalem—not that I had enough time, as I was only there for three weeks anyway. I practically cried and begged God to keep me in Jerusalem as I fell in love with the place. I did not want to go back to Dubai. But alas, as with all good times, they always end. I went to Jerusalem single and left the City of Gold still a single woman.

I may not have found somebody in Jerusalem; that was just wishful thinking from the start, but I sure was grateful for the opportunity to have finally seen the Promised Land. And looking back, I'm also glad that I didn't meet anyone with potential because I am quite happy with what God eventually gave me. I also know my husband and I are together today because we were both obedient. I could have rebelled and insisted on staying in Israel. My husband could have disobeyed and insisted on his own ways. But no, we both were willing to follow God's ways, no matter how hard and painful they were at times. We were both willing for God to work through us and in us. If we weren't obedient and submissive to God's will for our lives, we wouldn't have each other today.

If I had never tried online dating, my husband and I would probably still be single, living our separate lives in separate states, if not different continents. Worse, we could have settled for somebody less. Yes, like you, I also had my doubts at first. I was scared and embarrassed. But I learned to overcome my baseless fears and concerns. Online dating definitely requires an open mind. So, the question is, do you have an open or closed mind? Do you have preconceived notions about online dating? Even if you did, are you willing to give them up? You have to have the willingness to follow the leading of the Holy Spirit, even if it means stepping out of your comfort zone. Be willing to venture into the un-known; the unfamiliar. Or take the road less traveled even if it means being ostracized by friends and/or churchmates who don't agree with you.

Think about all the possibilities. Will your life be better if you try online dating and meet someone you like? What if the kind of person you have been waiting for and praying for all this time is on the other side of the screen? Will you not try it? Or would you prefer to wait and hope that someday, somebody will come knocking on your door? What if nobody comes? Will you continue to wait? What if you insist on waiting and ignore that gentle prodding of the Holy Spirit and miss out on somebody truly amazing online? Please weigh your options seriously. The answer to whether online dating is for you or not depends entirely on you. Check your attitude towards online dating. Count the costs. Consider your options. Pray. Then decide and act. Don't wait. Your future depends on it.

4

⧞

Debunking the Myth—Is Online Dating a Sin?

"Maricel, say, you go online and create a dating profile. What do you think is your priority?"

This was the point-blank question *John (name changed to protect his identity), from my church in Dubai, asked me without warning. I was sitting across from him at their dinner table. His wife *Mary (name changed to protect her identity), had invited me over for dinner numerous times previously, and I had repeatedly declined. But it reached a point where I had run out of excuses, so I finally said yes. I had no idea there was a sinister plot behind the invite. I felt trapped, with no way out.

The question came out of nowhere, so I was really taken by surprise. My jaw dropped as John's insinuations dawned on me. I could not believe my ears. Thoughts swirled in my head. "Was the man actually accusing me of prioritizing online dating over God by simply creating an online profile?" The realization hit me like a bucket of cold water.

A few months prior to the dinner, Mary confronted me at church one day. I was enjoying my Irish friend's wedding when Mary purposely crossed my path to chat with me. She initially asked how my life was, something she hadn't done in a while. I wanted to tell her that life wasn't going well. I was having medical issues and had been in and out of hospitals and clinics for almost a year. My work environment had turned toxic, and it was a struggle to go to work every day. Church was my only outlet, so I was more than happy to be there and celebrate. Mary had no idea about my struggles as I had tried to avoid her as much as I could. She had a proclivity to be tactless, and harsh words were the last thing I needed, given my physical and emotional state.

To keep our conversation short, I simply told Mary I was good and proceeded to walk away. Unfortunately, that did not deter her. Mary quickly threw down the gauntlet to me by revealing that she and John had been discussing my online dating affairs. And that they both concluded that I was desperate. I wasn't sure if it was her words that cut me to pieces or the way she uttered them that truly shocked me. I was too dazed to react. I was pretty sure Mary saw how the faint smile on my face suddenly vanished. I honestly couldn't remember what I said next.

I do remember wanting to avoid the couple for good, but I knew I could not. At least not yet. I wanted to say so many ugly things, but I chose to bite my tongue. I promised myself I would never walk into their trap again as I stepped away. But I obviously failed, as I found myself back at their table that night, several months after our encounter at the wedding.

What hurt me more was the fact that John and Mary were two of the people I had previously trusted and respected. I valued their opinion. We shared several meals and exciting adventures together. We had a good relationship for a few years. Please understand that I am in no way disparaging them. That is not my intention. I knew their misplaced reaction had more to do with their cultural background and age than their personalities. In their minds, they thought they could say whatever they wanted without being questioned.

I do believe their intentions were good; only their methods were flawed. So, when John confronted me at their table that night, I knew he thought he was doing me a favor. He probably believed he was trying to correct me and my errant ways. But nothing could be further from the truth. There was nothing wrong with what I was doing, and I knew what my priorities were. I also knew that my heart was right before God.

What John didn't know was that the time I spent online was nothing compared to the time I spent at church or in church activities. My online presence was intermittent. My online dating account was off for months at a time. I was too busy with church activities to even stay online for an hour. Unfortunately, people tend to draw their conclusions before verifying the information they're given. John made his assumptions simply based on what his wife, Mary, had told him—the same person who knew nothing about what was really going on with my life. Mary often asked about my love life and hardly asked about my prayer life or walk with God. I often wondered why. I had no idea she was trying to prove her point to her husband. To think that we only chatted for five minutes every time she cornered me at church. I never understood how she came up with that bizarre conclusion.

If I were desperate for a relationship, why did I recently break up with someone I met in person? Both John and Mary knew about that guy. Insulted, I flatly told John no, that he was wrong. John quickly realized the change in my tone. He knew that the conversation at his table was not going the way he expected it to. I told him bluntly that his thought process was flawed and that considering online dating a sin was unbiblical. I cited other couples from our church who met online and got married. John and Mary knew these couples, and they both approved of them. Did the couples sin when they dated online?

He knew he had gotten caught in his own trap, so he quickly denied it. He tried to deflect by saying he was just concerned that I was creating an online dating profile, as if it were a crime. John further stated that he wished I would find someone in person. I told him I agreed, but there was nothing wrong with finding someone online, either. And if nothing was happening in person, was it wrong for me or others to look online? John then bragged about couples who met in person at church and have since gotten engaged.

I told him I was happy for them, but it didn't mean I wouldn't find someone great online either. I wasn't even impressed with the people whose love lives John was so proud of, but I didn't say anything. I knew that some people at church often brag about couples whose genuine characters they seemingly can't see. Only to find them unraveling later before their very eyes, and it was too late to rectify the situation. I thought it clearly demonstrated an astonishing lack of discernment in all parties involved. But I also knew if I said something, people like John and Mary would think I was out of line. Or that I was simply jealous of the other couples.

I left the couple's place with a bad taste in my mouth. The Bible does not even mention dating anywhere, so how did they arrive at their egregious conclusion that online dating was a sin? The Bible does provide us with clear guidelines on what to look for in a spouse. Clearly, God does not care about how or where we meet our spouse, as long as it's not in some ungodly place like a bar. In contrast, God does care about one's character—in other words, the who. "But the Lord said unto Samuel, Look not on his countenance, or on the height of his stature; because I have refused him: for the Lord seeth not as man seeth; for man looketh on the outward appearance, but the Lord looketh on the heart." (1 Samuel 16:7)

If people lack discernment, it is no wonder they are so easily deceived. If people don't hear from God, it is no wonder they easily fall prey to men's manipulative ways. I cannot and will never agree with John's or anyone's insinuation that online dating is a sin. Never. I knew where I stood. And if any pastor or preacher told you otherwise, I can assure you that they are "prophe-lying". The Word of God is our ultimate guide. If what someone says is in the Bible or aligns with the Word of God, then you should believe it. But if it's not in the Bible or is the opposite of what the Word says, then take it with a grain of salt. Better yet, forget about it completely. It doesn't matter whether it's a well-known pastor or an elder talking. They are not the authorities; God and His Word are. Be sure to always refer to the Bible before believing what you're told. Pray for discernment. Pray that the Lord will open your spiritual eyes and ears so no one can deceive you.

It was painful to see my friendship with John and Mary decline, but I thought it was best for all of us. If I had tried to correct them, they would have taken it the wrong way. They were much older than I was, so I was sure they would not have taken it well. They did not deter me from reactivating my online dating profile, though. In fact, it only motivated me to prove them wrong. They also made me realize how totally out of sync we were in terms of online dating. I did not know it then, but I realized much later that there was a great need to address such misconceptions. This is also one of the things that prompted me to write this book. If some people at church consider online dating a sin, what hope is there for people inside the church who want to try it? What if they have not had any good experiences with in-person dating?

Are they supposed to conform to the norm that doesn't work and wait all their lives for possibly nothing? Or will they be "forgiven" and accepted like we do those who try traditional dating? To me, the question was never "how." The real question was "who." Who was I dating? What kind of man was I talking to? Is he a fellow believer? Is he a man, or is he living an alternative lifestyle? Is he marriage material, or is he the kind who can't keep or maintain a relationship? Does he have a stable job, or has he not held one in years? What is his character like? What is his prayer life like? Is he a member of a church, or does he church-hop? These are questions that truly matter. How or where you meet a person is immaterial compared to what kind of man or woman you are dating or considering. That should be everyone's primary focus, especially yours.

I can only hope that you can rest assured by now that there is nothing morally wrong with online dating. To say otherwise is a big mistake and has no biblical bearing whatsoever. I know a Christian couple who met on Facebook, and they are still happily married. Another Christian couple met on Friendster several years ago, and they are still married today. A handful of churchmates of mine met online and are still together. According to an article by Increditools, 14% of those who met online ended in matrimony. (Increditools, 2023) That means there are thousands of couples out there who met online and got married.

According to a study published by the University of Chicago, couples who met online are happier, and their marriages last longer. (Harms, 2013) Over 19,000 people participated in the survey, with 30 to 39 being the highest age bracket represented. The study showed a 6 percent marriage breakup among those who met online, whereas 7.6 percent was among those who met offline. A recent study also indicates that those who met online were not as likely to end in divorce. (Heimel et al., 2020) This is largely attributed to what I also mentioned in another chapter: the level of intentionality of online dating app users that may be lacking in some who date offline.

When I was single, other single ladies often complained about how unintentional single men from the church were. This was a common refrain among single ladies, even from other churches. Men seemingly like to hang out without saying a word, so they leave a lot of women wondering if they are really interested or are they just enjoying their company. Or, the men will look and stare but never make the approach, as if they were expecting the women to initiate. On the other hand, online users are serious about looking for genuine and lasting relationships. They know what they want; they pursue it, and they stick to it. The Knot 2019 Jewelry and Engagement study indicated 22 percent of those who met online got engaged. (OUTvoices, 2022)

Renowned theologian and author John Piper was asked a similar question, and he had a very powerful and profound response. According to him, the how is immaterial, but who you marry is what matters. (Piper, 2014) I couldn't agree more. 1 Timothy 3:2 gives us a glimpse of what to look for in an overseer. But if you look closer, there's so much you can glean from it in terms of what to look for in a potential man of the house: blameless, the husband of one wife, vigilant, sober, of good behavior, given to hospitality, apt to teach, and the list goes on. The Bible does not prohibit us from (online) dating per se, nor does it promote it. It only suggests that it's okay to take advantage of it. It's totally up to you. But it does give us a window into the character or qualities of a man (or woman) that we should be looking for. Above all, Paul exhorts us that an overseer (or a man) should be above reproach. That's the kind of man (or woman) we should be eyeing, whether online or offline.

5

Is Online Dating Worth the Risk?

To answer this question, you have to ask yourself a set of other questions. How much do you really want to get married? Meaning, how serious are you about getting married? Or is marriage just an afterthought for you? It's something nice to have, but you'll be okay if it does not happen. How often do you think about marriage? Is it something you think about today but then forget about tomorrow? Or is it something that you often think about? Or do you want marriage so much that you'll never be truly happy unless you're married? I ask you this specific question because it was true for me. I realized it at the most unexpected time and place.

I once had an opportunity to stay in the world's most luxurious hotel located in Dubai. My Indonesian friend was with me when I checked in. I asked her to accompany me, as I didn't want to spend the night in the hotel alone. After thoroughly enjoying the hotel's facilities and a sumptuous dinner in another luxurious hotel next door, my friend and I went to bed at around midnight. But as the darkness quickly gobbled up the evening lights and an eerie quiet descended upon us, I suddenly found myself sobbing. It was totally unexpected. Even I was surprised by my own emotional roller coaster. My friend was sound asleep as I lay in bed next to her. I was enjoying the utmost comfort and luxury I had never experienced before. And yet, there I was, overcome with more sadness than I could fathom.

That was when it dawned on me that no amount of luxury could ever take the place of my future husband. I thought I would rather live in a humble abode with my husband than live in a castle without a spouse. It was also then that I realized I could never be truly happy until I was married. I knew without a doubt that I was meant to be with someone. It was a turning point in my life, a poignant moment, so to speak, that I will never forget. Have you had a similar experience? Have you had a stirring moment in your life when you realized that you truly need a partner in life? Do you travel a lot for your job but always find yourself alone in a hotel and wish you weren't? Maybe you have been attending Christian conferences or events all over the country, but you often leave feeling desolate because you haven't met anybody.

Are you at the top of your career but still experiencing loneliness because you know something or somebody is missing? Are you doing something you really love but wish you were with your life partner? If only. Or you're somebody who knows deep down in your heart that you're meant to be married. If you answered yes to some or most of these questions, then maybe you do need to consider your options. No one but you can truly know what you need with the Holy Spirit's guidance. Dig deep into the Word of God, pray, and fast if you have to, to find out if marriage is really God's plan for you. Knowing this will help you determine whether on-line dating is truly worth the risk for you or not. There's no point in taking the risk if you're not even remotely interested in getting married.

I am cognizant of the fact that there are people out there who are genuinely happy being single, so you really have to know for yourself what you want. If you don't, then you're in trouble. If you do feel that you're really meant to be married, an even bigger question to ask yourself is why. Why do you want to get married? Is it for selfish reasons, or is it to serve and glorify God together? Do you know your purpose and understand that you can't achieve it without your husband (or wife)? Are you preparing yourself for that same purpose now? Are you preserving yourself for the same reason? Or are you expecting your future spouse to meet all your needs? A lot of people have a misaligned expectation that their future spouse will make them happy and meet all their needs. I think that is totally unrealistic and that they are setting themselves up for failure. It is also unfair to your future spouse.

Most often than not, people want to be with someone they're not. For example, some men want women who have never known men before, and vice versa. However, these same men who want a pure wife have a lascivious lifestyle. Some women want men who are financially secure so they don't have to work. Yes, sometimes it works out that way, but not always. What if you are this kind of woman and you meet a man who is of truly noble character but doesn't have much to offer? Are you going to let him go simply because you want your own financial needs met above all else? Again, character trumps any financial or physical needs. When I married my husband five years ago, all we owned were two old cars. Yes, he co-owned houses and land with his sisters. But I had no claim to any of it.

People expected me to marry a white guy with a big title and lots of money. Instead, I married a black guy who's a teacher, which is not a high-paying job. He is not an engineer, lawyer, or doctor. But I was never driven by money. I've always looked at a man's character. Yes, I've had admirers with titles, fancy cars, and nice houses. But they were inconsequential to me if their character was flawed. Or if they didn't have a relationship with God. I've traveled all over the world and met thousands of men; Cantrell was the very first man I've met who was a total package. Not only did he possess the character I had been looking for, but our beliefs were also complementary. Not to mention that he also dressed well, and we shared similar interests, including the symphony. The orchestra or the opera is not every man's cup of tea, so finding someone who shared that interest with me was a huge plus to boot.

I have always believed that the material aspect of a marriage can always follow. Most people only look at the present and cannot imagine the future. But if you are willing to put in the work, who's to say that the empty-handed person in front of you today is not going to be wealthy tomorrow? Remember, you should not despise the small beginnings, as

Zechariah 4:10 warns us. Do not be blinded by the material stuff; they will quickly fade away. However, a man's character is there to stay. What will you do with all the wealth if the man (or woman) you're married to does not respect you? I see this inside and outside the church all the time. It's a very disappointing and painful sight at the same time. That is not how God designed marriage to be.

So, don't be afraid to take a chance with someone who does not currently meet your financial needs. Let the Holy Spirit lead you. The two of you can always build your future together. Just be willing to work with your spouse. Be willing to work for your future. Five years in, my husband and I have come a long way from owning practically nothing together to owning our home and newer vehicles. From struggling to go on date nights to dining in fancy restaurants whenever we want. From not being able to travel far to flying anywhere, anytime we want. We are still a long way from where we want to be, but at least we've progressed. Just because you don't have much today doesn't mean you'll always be lacking or wanting. No. If you're a true child of God, He will provide ALL your needs, as He promises in Philippians 4:19.

If there's one takeaway from the hundreds of books I've read about relationships, it's this: be the person your future spouse will need. Stop expecting and start preparing. That's the best thing you can do for him (or her) now. If you want financial stability, then be willing to work and save. Do not expect your future husband to do all the work and all the saving for you. Marriage is a partnership, so don't put all the pressure on your future spouse. I do not regret traveling all over the world, but I did wish that I had saved more. Be happy if you find a man who's already financially stable. But be thankful, too, if God brings you someone who has the right character but doesn't have much materially. As long as you two agree, abundance will flow eventually.

So, if you know you're really meant to be married and you're open to God's plans for you, then online dating might be worth the risk for you. But unless you're fully committed, you will give up online dating as soon as you encounter a hump. Online dating will be a chore rather than an exciting adventure to enjoy. You will not see it as an essential platform to meet your future spouse someday. Instead, you will treat it as a nuisance, something that is in the way of your busy schedule. I know this for a fact. I know some who have this lopsided attitude towards online dating. They tried online dating for a while, but because their hearts were not in it, they gave up at the first sign of trouble. Some just had wrong or misaligned expectations. As soon as the men they met behaved in certain ways they did not expect, they blocked them. Or refused to talk to them anymore.

Online dating needs to be treated as you would in-person dating. You cannot expect a person to act differently online from the men or women you date in person. Just because it's online dating, it does not mean everything happens overnight. It takes as much time and patience as it does in person. Unfortunately, the people I knew had a totally different understanding. They were too impatient and wanted the men to move sooner rather than later. They did not have the time to wait, or so they claimed. The problem was, they had already waited all their lives, so what was wrong with waiting another month or two? These women were okay with waiting on men they met in person, but for some reason, they weren't willing to wait on men they met online.

You cannot expect a complete stranger to propose in just one month. Only scammers do that. Make sure you do not have unrealistic expectations, as some of my peers did. If anything, you need to be more patient with someone you meet online than in person. You'll need to give more time to let the relationship develop and grow. Besides, you cannot be too careful these days. The internet is rife with frogs and impostors. Spend more time getting to know each other. Start out as friends. Yes, the primary goal is to find a potential mate. But there is no law against starting out as friends either. Friendship is the fundamental foundation of any relationship, so enjoy it. A lot of my peers didn't want to start as friends either, which is why their attempts were doomed to fail from the beginning.

So, going back to the question, is online dating worth the risk? It sure is if you really want to find a partner in life. Just look at my husband and me. I can say unequivocally that he sure was worth the risk. Just before flying to Shreveport to meet Cantrell's family, my youngest sister asked me, "Are you not scared?" I didn't bother to ask her what she meant. I could interpret her question in so many ways. Was I not scared that I was meeting my boyfriend's family alone? Was I not scared of being in a strange city, etc.? I didn't care. I appreciated that my sister was concerned, but I didn't want to entertain any doubts in my mind because I knew what I was getting into. I knew that I had found a diamond in the rough. I knew that I had found the most amazing man ever. For the first time in my life, I felt certain about a man, and I was not going to let him go unless the Lord Himself told me to, which, thankfully, He did not.

I just have to look at other married couples I know who met online, and it makes it worth it. I also just have to look at the sheer number of closed-minded women I know who are still single today, and I am thoroughly convinced online dating is worth the risk. No, I am not looking down on these women because they are single. That was their choice, if not their own doing. I have a problem with the reason they are still single because they mock people like me who dated online and got married. Because instead of taking encouragement from my experience and success story, they resent me while inadvertently fanning the flame of jealousy. Not that I'm bothered by what they say about me. I have never been happier or felt more blessed. That's all I truly care about. I do feel sorry for them because the longer they resent me, the less likely they'll get married.

I knew the price that came with online dating and obeying God's call in my life. I expected that it wouldn't be smooth sailing either. When I obeyed God's call to move to the United States, I was ready to be poor and lonely. Instead, God has blessed me tremendously, with my husband as the greatest gift of all since I left everything behind. Yes, as I plainly illustrated, there is a price to be paid. There will be talks behind your back by people you used to call sisters and brothers in the Lord. There will be snickers, disappointments, and mockeries. But they really are petty compared to the astounding joy you will possibly experience if and when you do find your true love online. That alone should make online dating worth the risk, right?

One other question you should ask is, "Are there any available men (or women) around you physically?" I am a firm believer that God brings us prospects, but it is up to us to decide who to marry, not God. Do you have a current suitor who might check all the boxes? Do you like someone who might make a suitable marriage partner? The fact that you're reading this, the answer is probably no. I've been there, done that. A lot of single women once surrounded me, with only a handful of single men around. I did not know anyone with whom I was truly compatible. I've had crushes, but as soon as I got to know them a little better, I realized they weren't exactly who I thought they were. That made my options even more limited. So, if you are in the same situation as I was before, perhaps it's really time to reconsider your options. Take a long, hard look at the possibilities. Because if you don't, you might remain single for a really long time. Is that really the kind of risk you're willing to take?

It's one thing to wait if you're in your early 20s. You do have plenty of time left, maybe. But if you're already in your late 30s, 40s, or 50s, there's no reason for you to dilly-dally. We all wish God would work according to our timetables. Psalm 31:15 clearly declares that our time is in God's hands, not the other way around. We also wish that God would do things our way. But Isaiah 55:8–9 clearly says, "For my thoughts are not your thoughts, neither are your ways my ways, saith the Lord. For as the heavens are higher than the earth, so are my ways higher than your ways, and my thoughts than your thoughts." Clearly, we cannot make God move fast enough. But God does give us the wisdom and tools necessary to live out our purpose on earth. It is up to us to use and take advantage of the tools that God provides. If it can help fulfill our destiny, why not? If online dating sites can help us find who God wants us to be with, why not use them?

Stop limiting God by putting Him in a box. If in-person dating hasn't worked out for you in years, if not decades, it must be time to try something new. I'm not saying that a woman should pursue a man. You may or may not agree, but I believe it's a man's job to pursue a woman. Not the other way around. I'm merely suggesting that you make yourself available in ways and places where God is seemingly working. Just because you've never tried online dating doesn't mean it's wrong and you shouldn't give it a try. In the same way, just because online dating worked for someone does not necessarily mean it's going to work for you, either. All I'm saying is that you have to give it a try. And it's worth giving it a try.

All that God wants from us is our faith and obedience. Do you believe God can use something as unconventional as online dating to bring people together? If so, then go and take a gander. Do you believe that anything is possible with God? Then what are you waiting for? I, too, had to overcome my fears and concerns. It scared me that someone I knew in person might accidentally discover my online dating account. But then again, I had to ask myself, "So what?" It's none of their business. And it's my love life, not theirs, that's at stake. I had to focus only on what I needed and not on what others might think or say. And I am so grateful that I found the courage to try it that day. I should say I thank God for giving me the courage to do it.

After three years of turning my profile on and off, I eventually met my husband-to-be online. He, too, had been online for seven years before we met. He, too, had had several setbacks online and offline and was ready to settle when we met. And because we both set aside our pride and concerns about online dating, since meeting, we have been smiling from ear to ear every day. No more tears at night. No more crying to God for our spouses. God surely turned our sorrows into joy. Online dating was sure worth the risk, and we have not regretted it since. So, if you're at the end of your rope and feel like giving up in-person dating altogether, please don't throw in the towel yet.

Hold on tight a little longer. You will never know what you will find out if you never try it. You will never know what's on the other side of the computer screen if you never go on-line. If you've truly been seeking and praying for a potential mate, online dating is a door that's wide open for you today. All you have to do is walk through it. God may open doors for you, but it is up to you to walk through them. But if you never do, then you will never find out what awaits you on the other side. Take a step forward today, and maybe, just maybe, your life's greatest adventure yet is about to begin.

6

⚜

Is Finding Love Online Better Than Finding Love Offline?

Is finding love online better than finding love offline or in real life? It all depends. This is one of those tricky questions that cannot be answered with a simple yes or no. The answer often depends entirely on your experience(s) with the opposite sex in real life. If your experience with dating in person has always been good, then there's probably no need for you to even consider online dating. However, if your in-person experiences have not been stellar, then you should definitely consider online dating as an option. Who knows, it might prove to be an even better option for you as it turned out to be for my husband and me.

Remember that whether online or offline, men will all be

the same. They will have their flaws and shortcomings, just like everybody else. Be sure to lower your expectations but not your standards. Factor in the possibility that you will be disappointed online as much as you will be offline. Maybe more, maybe less. I can never promise that online dating will be better for you than in-person dating. All I can say is that it is worth trying, and it will be up to you to judge whether it's better or worse. I can only share my personal experiences and those of others' I have personally witnessed. I can say that they were pretty much the same. In the beginning, at least.

Both have their advantages and disadvantages. Both gave me disappointments and frustrations. But if I only zoom in on the result, I can definitely say online dating is much better, simply because that is how I met my amazing husband. That said, your answer to this question will definitely rely not just on your encounters on the platforms but on the actual outcome of your experience. That is, if you'd be willing to stay online long enough to find out. I say this because I've seen far too many people try for a little while and give up. Like anything in life worth having, it is worth fighting for. If you want to succeed in online dating, you must be willing to invest time and energy, or probably even money if you opt for a paid dating site. The choice is entirely yours.

Prior to meeting my husband, there was only one other man I seriously considered and prayed about. Two at the most, but the other one was an old friend I often fought with in college. Had we ended up with each other, it would have been a massive train wreck. And the fault would not have been solely his. Besides, I was too young at the time to understand my emotions and what was going on with me. The other one I got really close to was a friend with whom I got entangled in what seemingly looked like a love (emotional) triangle. We were good friends at the beginning, sharing our lives over healthy fellowships and adventures with others.

However, things quickly took a turn among the three of us when a common female friend started insinuating that our male friend was interested in her. But our male friend was hanging out exclusively with me at the time but not with her. She was never on his lips when he was with me, but he was always on her lips. She often pretended and denied liking our friend whenever I asked her. But then she'd also deflect and start sharing about what our male friend did or said to her implying that he was into her. I believed she often denied her feelings for our common male friend whenever I asked her because she knew that the guy and I were hanging out. But the stories she told were almost believable and planted serious doubts and fears in me. I started wondering about what our male friend's real intention towards me was. If he was hanging out with other women while hanging out with me, what was he doing and why?

The last thing I wanted was to be a "meantime" friend. You know, someone enjoys your company and that of others' while waiting for the right woman (or man), with no regard for your emotions. I thought I did not wait a lifetime to end up like that to someone. So, I quickly hatched a plan to end my friendship with our common male friend. I know. It sounds rash. But for someone who was in the habit of sabotaging potential relationships due to her insecurities and fears stemming from her dark past, it was "normal" for me. Yes, I was already a believer, but as it turned out, I had not yet been completely delivered from my past. To cut a long story short, I did sabotage my friendship with the male friend in the hopes of paving the way for the female friend. Things also started to get toxic between the female friend and me. I was just grateful not to get entangled in such an unhealthy web of friendship anymore.

I failed to do one thing, though. I didn't bother to clarify things with our male friend first before I sabotaged things between him and me. I didn't factor in his feelings or the fact that he might have truly valued me and my friendship. Also, he was a brother-in-Christ first before he was a friend. Suffice to say, without getting into details, he made it known that I hurt him very badly. I learned not to blame the woman, either. She was just a woman wanting a man, a woman who was willing to do or say anything to keep a man by her side. Don't get me wrong; I too was hurt so badly. It wasn't easy at all. In fact, the next few years were the most painful years of my life, as the Lord used the opportunity to work His way in and through me.

This experience with my male friend showed me how petty and unprepared I was for a relationship with any man, even a mere friendship. Although I will always regret the way I ended my association with my male friend, I am grateful that God didn't waste it. God exposed the darkness of my heart and showed me what was really going on deep within. Thankfully, after over five years of not seeing each other, my old male friend and I had a chance to catch up and reconcile. Seeing him one last time, with him wishing to see me again afterwards, gave me the closure that I needed. Reconciling with my male friend made me realize I was finally ready for a real relationship with a good man.

But even before reconciling with my male friend, I actually had one "fake" relationship with a man. Oddly enough, we met in person at a church event in Florida. The man was at least 10 years older than I was. I thought his age meant he was mature and wise. I was in for a shock. He knew I had never been in a relationship before, but instead of treasuring me, he quickly took advantage of my naiveté. He was well respected at church, and he was well mannered. But it was all a front. Soon, he was making more promises than he would ever deliver. He seemingly knew the Bible well, so it quite baffled me why he kept making promises he had no intention of keeping. His actions (or inactions) were exactly the opposite of what the Bible said. I really didn't know why I kept forgiving him, either. In just two months, he turned from what I thought was a total package to a total jerk. I never imagined a man would have no qualms about professing to be a Christian while behaving exactly the opposite.

I felt like a fool, no doubt. He had a fake charm that I regretted falling for. People used to tell me that not all men who claim to be Christians are Christians, and they were right. It was a hard lesson learned, and a hard pill to swallow at that. It was a trap I thought I would never fall for, but I sure did. Our fake "relationship," if you could even call it that, lasted only a few months. I was so wrong about him. And I hope you can learn from this lesson. That such a man had stayed single for so long was a clear red flag. I am not saying it is always the case, but it usually is. It is typically a sign of fear of commitment. He was either too picky for the right reasons or simply enjoying his freedom to mingle with whomever, with no strings attached. I believed it was the latter. I thought he was ready to commit, but I was clearly wrong about him. I thank God every day now that I did not end up with him. Still, I wish our fake relationship had never happened at all.

But now that I know what true love really is, I realize I never really loved the guy. It was pure infatuation. I thought I had finally met a self-made man. But all is well that ends well. So, I remind you again, ladies (or gents), what Song of Solomon 8:4 warns us against: "I charge you, O daughters of Jerusalem, that ye stir not up, nor awake my love, until he please." To him, it was all a farce, so even today, I still consider my husband my first boyfriend. So, you see, I really had no in-person dating experience that I can be proud of. Most of the men who pursued me were ungodly, so I never really considered them either. Yes, I've had crushes in between, even one that lasted six years. But he was quite happy being single, so I decided to move on. And I was right, because he is still single today.

A few other Christian men tried, but I knew none of them was the right guy for me, so I didn't give them a chance. I never believed in wasting my or someone else's time just to pass the time. Unfortunately, not everybody, even Christian men (and women), has the same mindset. In fact, Cantrell was the first man I've met who had the same thinking as I did. This is actually what prompted me to try online dating. Since I didn't have a lot of notable experiences in person, the only other choice was online. And I thank God for giving people the wisdom to create avenues like online dating for people like me. I knew I needed help connecting with the right kinds of men, so I honestly do not know where I would be today without online dating.

Yes, it's possible I would have gotten married eventually, but most probably unhappy. I may have made the biggest relationship blunder of my life with my male friend, but God turned it around and made something beautiful out of it. God traded my ashes for His beauty. I learned so much about myself and all the things I needed to give up, let go of, and repent of. How about you? Do you have any personal experiences that would convince you that in-person dating is better or worse? Or did you already have encounters online that convinced you that online dating is better or worse? If you have no experience in either, perhaps it's time to open your heart to God and ask for His leading.

Regardless of what avenue you choose to take, there is no right or wrong path. Either way is okay. I can only hope that whatever path you choose will be the right one. Or that it does lead you to the right person. It doesn't matter if you choose both. To me, that's just a sign of complete surrender. You are not choosing for yourself; you are allowing God to show Himself faithful to you as you make yourself open to His ways. Being open to His ways is a sign of surrender. And there is nothing more aromatic to God than a life fully surrendered to Him and His ways. Let Him work His ways in you and experience the wonders that await.

7

Pros and Cons of Online Dating

Like many things in life, there are pros and cons, advantages and disadvantages, and drawbacks. The same way with online dating. The good thing is you do not have to face them all alone. In this chapter, I outline and unpack the pluses and minuses of online dating for you so you can make an informed decision about whether to try online dating or not. At least, that's my hope. Let's start with the positive things first.

The Pros

No second guessing: Unlike in real life, when you're on an online dating site, everybody's motive is clear. There is no second-guessing. This was my biggest struggle with the few men I went out with. I was not sure if we were friends or simply out enjoying the day or night. Or were we friends on a date? Just like what happened with me and my friend who was hanging out with me in the preceding chapter. Since I was too naïve and afraid to ask, I didn't like not knowing the answer. I hated the thought of being a "meantime" friend. Was my friend going out with me to enjoy his time while waiting for the right girl? Or was he spending time with me to get to know me and see if there was any potential for us to be together in the future? I just didn't know.

Granted, I should have dared ask him instead of systematically sabotaging what might have been happening. But how do you ask a man, especially a friend, without looking or sounding too bold or aggressive? I had no clue. I was too shy around men with great potential. As an Asian woman, and a Filipina at that, it was never our place to ask the man first. We were expected to wait until the man expressed his feelings for us. Or wait forever for nothing. Or just move on. At least, that was how it was in my generation. I don't really know what it's like now. To compound the matter, waiting was something I was just never good at. I really struggled with being left wondering all the time, to the point where I made up my mind to never get close to another man unless I was sure of his intentions. Thankfully, there was online dating.

With online dating, you don't even need to ask whether you're dating or not. It's crystal clear at the outset. Nobody can say or pretend that you were just passing time. If you first met online and agreed to meet in person, you know the intention is clear. You're going out to get to know each other and see what the future might hold for you, if any. There may be no strings attached, but you both know what the motivations are. You can also lay your cards on the table at the very beginning about what your expectations are. Or what you hope to achieve during the meetup. It might take weeks, or months, but at least you know that both your intentions are clear.

The last thing you want is to get close to a man without knowing what his intentions are. I have seen this happen more often than not. Unfortunately, a man can spend much time with a woman without getting attached. Not so with women. Women are emotional and get attached easily. I've seen this firsthand with my male friend and other people too. As we spent time together exclusively and in groups, I could see myself getting drawn to him. That was how our other female acquaintances fell for him. None of them expected it, but that's the thing. You just never know what might happen when two hearts collide. This is why it's never a good idea for a married person (or even a single person) to hang out exclusively with someone of the opposite sex. So please play it safe, always. Unfortunately, not all men (or women), even those who claim to be Christians, see things this way.

This was actually what set my husband, Cantrell, apart from other men. When I first met Cantrell, this was one of the first few things we talked about. We quickly realized that we both had the same standards and philosophies in life. We both believed that if you already knew that a man (or woman) was not for you, why waste his (or her) time? He, too, had an admirer (on top of many others) for almost 30 years, but he never once asked her out. Never once did he go out with her for a meal; never once did he watch a movie with her. Not even in groups. He understood what a man could do to a woman if he spent time with her. So, he was very careful not to lead the woman on, or any other woman, for that matter. He did not like to leave a woman in suspense, either. He quickly stopped pursuing a woman if he felt that the Holy Spirit wanted him to let go.

Like me, he only dated a few. He was very intentional and clear about his motives each time. I believe you can better show you care about someone by not leading them on. Spending time exclusively with them is never a wise thing. If you are lonely, spend time with someone of the same sex— another man (or woman). Never with the opposite sex. That is the rule of thumb you must follow. Even at our former church in Shreveport, they encouraged us to hang out only with other married couples. I thought that was wise advice. The point is, it's so easy to get attached to someone and develop feelings for someone you spend time with often. Some might say this is an extreme measure. But this can really save a lot of heartaches if followed. I've seen marriages fall apart and relationships shattered over something that started off small or innocent.

You can ask the right questions freely: During the first few months of my time online, I was still acting like I was talking to a man in person. I beat around the bush. I struggled to ask the right questions. I did not want to offend or drive a man away. But the more men I interacted with online, the more I realized that most of them were acting like a bunch of idiots. They asked the wrong questions or said the wrong things. Who offers the world or gives their heart to someone they've never met? Frustrated, I started asking tougher questions. I realized if they were who they said they were, then they wouldn't feel insulted. Or my questions won't offend them.

But if they were frauds, they would fall flat on their faces and get caught in their own lies.

This was how Cantrell first caught my attention. I fired tough questions at him right at the beginning, thinking he would pull a disappearing act on me, but he did not. Instead, he kept coming back, asking me equally tough questions. The more we interacted, the tougher the questions we fired at each other. And that's how it's supposed to be. Don't feel shy about asking the right and hard questions. I provide an extensive list of questions that you can ask in a separate chapter. That's the only way you can really get to know a person. That's also the only way you can weed out fraudsters. The nicer I was, the longer it took to see through a man. I only ended up wasting my own time. So, don't ever apologize for being tough. You will save a lot of time and effort if you do that. Only real (godly) men can handle tough questions. No need to waste time on ungodly men (or women).

You do it at your own pace: Another thing that I really like about online dating is that there is no rush. You can do it at your own pace. Since you're not talking in person, it's easier to protect and control your emotions. Your heart is always guarded (at least, you would think). You decide how soon you want to meet and where. I had only been talking to Cantrell for a few days, but by the second day, he was already thinking of visiting me in Florida. He was based in Shreveport, Louisiana, at the time. By the seventh day, he had practically dropped the bomb on me. He asked if he could visit me in Florida sometime soon. Now, this wasn't the first time I heard something similar, so I was skeptical. That's another thing you need to remember: men (or women) will tell you things you want to hear. So always be skeptical until you actually see proof that what they're saying is true.

Don't feel the need to rush. When Cantrell told me he was coming, I honestly didn't feel like I was ready to meet him. I just got burned by another man, so I knew I wasn't going to rush anything, even if I liked everything I saw about him so far. Thankfully, he didn't mean to visit right then. He actually needed to wait another month before he could see me. If I were you, I would really take the time to get to know someone. Wait it out if you need to; take a month, two, or three, however long it takes. If you're ready to meet in one week, then go for it too. You are the best judge of your readiness. As long as you follow the safety measures I outlined in this book, then you should be okay. And you can always take a break from online dating. Whenever I felt like I was getting overwhelmed, I often turned off my account for weeks. Sometimes even months. Again, feel free to break away at any time.

Step away when you feel like it. Go back online whenever you feel like you're ready for it. Online dating can be emotionally draining. When you see an interesting profile, you can easily get excited. But then, the man (or woman) might not reply or respond to you. Or they might just be taking their time away from the platform too. It's so easy to get excited online—as much as you can readily get disappointed. One moment you're on an emotional high, and the next minute you're down. So be prepared—not just emotionally but mentally. Make sure you have as much fun in person with friends as you do online. Do not let the online world take over your personal life. True love takes time. So, whether it takes you months or days to find somebody interesting online, do not be in a hurry. Do not force things to happen too. Take one day at a time.

And when you do find someone interesting, gauge each other's comfort level as to when to move from the platform to talking on the phone, to video chatting, and then to meeting in person. Remember, there is a time for everything. Cantrell and I moved from exchanging messages on the platform to phone numbers in a matter of days. Within the first week, we were already Skyping or video calling each other. We saw each other in person over a month later. Ours was a whirl-wind romance, but yours doesn't have to be. Or it can be too. Again, it all depends on your maturity level and readiness for a relationship. And, of course, if and when you think the person you're talking to online might be the right one for you or not. Always pray and ask the Holy Spirit to guide you each and every step of the way. God will be more than happy to be involved in your love life.

You have more control over the conversation: Since you're talking virtually, there is no need to impress each other. After all, you don't even know if that would be your last conversation, so why even try? Yes, you do try to look good on camera, but it's easier to dispel any attempts to impress verbally. Cantrell made no attempts to impress me. He was as transparent on camera as he was on email. We had lengthy discussions on dating, waiting, marriage, doctrines, etc. If I threw a hard question at him and he didn't have an answer at the time, he was honest enough to say he wasn't sure what to make of it. But he was willing to ponder it and get back to me later. I did the same. We talked about our varying takes on certain doctrines. He was willing to listen to where I was coming from, and vice versa.

When you're talking to somebody in person, it's easier to get intimidated or nervous and forget the questions you had lined up in your mind. It's also so much easier to get distracted by how he (or she) smells, how he (or she) is dressed, or how he (or she) talks. Or even by the surrounding people, the music being played where you are, and other external factors. Not necessarily so with online dating, so the conversation can be quite fluid. Or not. And if you don't like how or where the conversation is going, it's also totally up to you to end it. Just come up with an excuse that you had other things to do and that it was nice meeting them. Try to be polite always, and you don't have to talk to them ever again. It's entirely up to you if you want to give them a second or third chance.

You can ignore the men (or women) you don't like: Have you ever been pestered by admirers who wouldn't take no for an answer? It can get emotionally draining and mentally exhausting. Not so with online dating. Requests and messages from people who don't even meet your criteria will bombard you, trust me. But that's just life on the World Wide Web. Sadly, there are so many lonely people out there, and so many scammers, too. The great thing, though, is that it's so much easier to ignore them. They don't have your number, so all they can do is send you repeated requests. At least it's not as annoying as missed calls. All you have to do is ignore or skip their messages. You are in no way obligated to read their messages. They will eventually get it, and they'll stop reaching out to you. Or sometimes they don't. Just keep ignoring. That's the key.

They don't have your address, so they can't just show up at your door either. Have you ever had somebody show up at your door, and you couldn't seem to get them out of your place? Been there, done that. With online dating, you won't ever have to face this kind of problem. Unless, of course, you've already given the man (or woman) your address. If anybody tries to harass you online, you can just auto-delete their emails, ignore them, or block them. Some online dating apps allow you to submit someone's profile to be blocked by the admin. You can show how many emails you've gotten from a person, and they will quickly take care of it. So, if anybody's harassing you, no worries. It's so easy to fix. Unlike if it's in person, it's not so easy to handle.

Less opportunity for you to get hurt: Unless you're already deep in the dating scene with a man (or woman), it's so hard to get hurt online. If you hardly know the person, it's hard to fall head over heels for them, so it's less likely for you to get hurt. But if you meet somebody in person and you get to know each other deeply, getting hurt by that person when that relationship does not work out is more inevitable. Since I had a failed "fake" relationship in the past in person, I have learned to guard my heart well. Sometimes all too well. But that really served me well in the online dating scene. And to set the record straight, I was not devastated when our so-called "relationship" ended. I can't even say I was hurt, thank goodness. But I was disappointed in him as much as I was disappointed in myself. It disappointed me that I failed to see through him. It did bruise my ego because I thought I was spiritually mature enough to have known better.

When you're online, complete strangers will bombard you

with strange proposals. If you know who you are and are not gullible, you know it's better to ignore these kinds of men. They're nothing but trouble and are only after your money. They will send you rosy emails, hoping you will take the bait. If you're in a lonely and vulnerable place, it's easy to fall for such scammers. For that's all they are—scammers. So, my advice to you is to make sure that you are not going online when you are most vulnerable emotionally. Because you could easily fall headlong. This happens a lot to widows and older women. But if you are secure in yourself and you know who you are in Christ, this shouldn't be a problem for you.

If you inadvertently like a seemingly good potential man (or woman) and get rejected, it's much easier to forget that person and move on. As the saying goes, there are too many fish in the sea. The one that got away was just one in a million, more like billions. So, if you do get rejected, lift your head up, dust off your clothes, and move on. There is no point in crying over spilled milk. The fact that the person allowed you to fall through the cracks means he or she is not worthy of you. This was exactly my attitude when I dumped the older man. As far as I know, he's still single today, probably playing with another younger woman's emotions. Surely, the right man (or woman) for you will give you the attention you deserve. And he (or she) is there somewhere. At the right time and in the right place, the right kind of man (or woman) for you will cross paths with you one day. Just learn to trust God's timing.

The Cons

What about the cons? What are the disadvantages of

dating online? You might wonder. Are there any? Of course, there are many. There are a host of disadvantages to dating online, just as there are disadvantages to dating someone in person.

Lots of fraudsters/impostors: For one, you will have to sift through so many frogs before you can find a prince—if you do find one. Let me be clear: There is no guarantee that you will find your prince (or princess) online. For the three years that I was online, most of the time before my account was de-activated, I met countless fraudsters. It was a very frustrating experience. I could almost always detect whether the person was fake or not right away. But even those few that I thought were not turned out to be. The sadder part of it was that every one of them claimed to be Christians. Yes, I only talked to those who seemed to be genuine Christians. I was on a Christian dating site, after all.

After a while, I had to resign myself to the fact that people in America tend to use the label "Christian" loosely. I am not saying that this is prevalent only in America, but this was my experience with American men. I honestly didn't see this happen in Dubai, but I rarely interacted with men in Dubai or Europe online so I have no benchmark. Most of the "Christian" Americans I interacted with online didn't bat an eye over divorce, as if it were something so normal. Perhaps it really was. They had no qualms about sleeping around, either. That's why, by the time Cantrell reached out to me, I was so frustrated that I wanted him to go through the eye of the needle before I was going to give him my time of day.

So, if and when you do try to go online, be prepared to face many impostors. From my experience, there were more of them online than in person. Only because the virtual world kind of gave them a sense of power and immunity, it was easier to hide their identity behind the screen than in person. They wouldn't just approach you in real life but they would online. You can be sure to get so many requests from strangers from all over the world. Of course, you can always limit your search areas, but I will talk more about that in the online safety tips section. But just know that they will bombard you online way more than they would pester you in person. But if you're willing to take the risk, go for it. Just keep telling yourself that, in order to get to the best, you have to go through the worst. That's what I told myself over and over: that it was worth it. And as you already know, my patience did pay off.

I would randomly deactivate my account for months to get a breather. And when I felt loneliness creeping in again, I went back on. Or, when I felt I was ready to give online dating one more try, I checked out other men's profiles as I got bolder and bolder. I was no longer shy about sending smiles to men whose profiles I found interesting. Oh yeah. It was very rare, though. You can also "favorite" a man (or woman) to let them know that you find their profiles charming. It did not always work, but it did for some. Of course, you'll get a lot of men favoriting your profile too. You can return the favor or you don't have to. You can also see if a man (or woman) has viewed your profile and how many times. Some of them will never reach out to you, maybe out of fear or intimidation. Some eventually will. Just be patient. Let them come around on their own terms.

Incessant emails: One thing that totally took me by surprise about going online was the sheer number of emails and messages I received. It was unprecedented. I didn't know how to handle it or react at first. Eventually, I learned not to let the emails overwhelm me by ignoring the ones that came from men with unimpressive profiles. Before even opening someone's message, I always checked out the man's profile, and if I deemed he didn't fit the bill, I simply ignored it. In the beginning, I read all the emails, not wanting to miss anyone or anything. But I noticed that the sender gets notified once you read their email. So, if you read an email from somebody uninteresting, they will bug you constantly. They'll send you more emails asking why you're not replying, as if your actions or inactions weren't plain enough.

Unwanted attention: I was also shocked to receive numerous proposals, as in marriage proposals, from complete strangers. Young or old, it didn't matter. Single or separated, they were pouring in from everywhere. This was one of the deterrents that kept me on and off the online dating world. I was so frustrated until I finally learned to just shut them out. No matter how many times they bug you, just ignore them. Because the minute you reply, you will get flooded with more questions and unpalatable messages.

Hard to decipher the truth from the lie: If you're a Christian, as you most likely are, online dating requires a lot of discernment. Honestly, if you feel like you're too immature to discern who's telling the truth or not, I would highly discourage you from even trying to go online. The online world is riddled with scammers, catfishers, and phonies. If you're the unsuspecting type, it would be even harder for you to survive. Online dating is not for the faint-hearted, nor is it for the sensitive, or the onion-skinned. You have to be gutsy to ask tough questions. You have to dig deep. Don't settle for vague answers, or they'll keep you wondering. That's the only way you can distinguish the liars from the honest ones. The good thing about pathological liars is that they often fall into their own traps.

I remember meeting somebody who claimed to be a marketing executive. But the more I exchanged emails with him, the more I realized the guy could not even spell properly. So, that alone made me question whether the guy was actually a marketer or not. Then he couldn't get his stories straight. First, his mom got sick, so he apologized for the late reply. Then, in another email, it was a relative, not his mom, who got sick. He would email me on and off, and I got so tired of him that I tried blocking him. But I really didn't have much reason to block him except that he couldn't get his stories straight. That wasn't enough grounds to get a person blocked from contacting you. So, I had to put up with the man's incessant emails and excuses. Just like with other men that I got tired of, I simply learned to ignore him. It took two years, but he finally left me alone for good.

According to eHarmony, age, height/weight, and job/income are the top three things online dating users often lie about. The so-called marketing executive I mentioned earlier is definitely one of them. Using a much younger photo is all too common as well. I learned this the hard way. When the really good-looking guy I mentioned in the first chapter first contacted me, his photo took me by surprise. I almost fell off my chair. The guy was so handsome in his profile photo that I thought he should be an actor. But when I checked his age, it didn't match his photo. He looked like he was in his 20s, but his age suggested he was already in his 40s. Maybe he was reliving his glory days. Who knows?

Since the guy had other photos that were a little older, I gave him a pass. But when I finally met him in person, my heart sank. There was no trace of the good-looking and youthful glow on the man's face. The guy almost looked so ordinary I couldn't believe it was the same guy. He looked scraggly, with pockmarks on his face from acne. Don't get me wrong; he was still a little cute, but nothing close to what I saw in his photos. So never take anything online at face value. Triple-check, double-check, and always check. Do your research. Be on the alert. You never know what kind of man (or woman) you're talking to. Unfortunately, with this man, he also looked okay on camera. Maybe that's why he always had a dim light around him, so I couldn't see how old he really was compared to his profile photo. Not that I was focused on his appearance alone, but looks do matter, right?

It can be a dangerous place to be: The biggest drawback of dating online is that it can be a very dangerous place to be. Yes, if and only if you are not careful. Time and time again, you will hear of reports of teenagers falling prey to registered sex offenders they met online. Or about women not returning home alive after meeting someone they first met online. Or of sexual assault victims after coming face-to-face with the person they first met online.

There is also a significant uptick in sexual assaults related to online dating. (Lefroy, 2022) According to eHarmony, 40 million Americans are using online dating apps, and about 57% of users lie on their online dating profiles. (eHarmony, 2021) Moreover, one in ten adults in the U.S. gets scammed or defrauded every year. (Lazic, 2022) On the other hand, about two million people have already found love online on eHarmony alone. (eHarmony, n.d.) That includes my husband and me, although we met on a different dating platform. Granted, some of these figures can sound so frightening, but many of these things happen in person too. In fact, having your wallet snatched can more likely result in identity fraud than if you were surfing online. (Lazic, 2022) So, don't let these statistics scare you. If you follow the safety tips and take extra precautions, you shouldn't have to worry about falling prey to scams and whatnot. It is always good to be self-aware and remain vigilant, whether you are online or offline.

So, there you have it—the pros and cons of online dating. There are other things I have not mentioned, but that's for you to find out. Nothing should stop you from doing your own research. You need to carefully weigh all the advantages and disadvantages of online dating. You will have to decide for yourself whether it's worth the risk or not. And if you decide to try it, I provide online safety tips in the succeeding chapter. If you follow all, if not most of them, I see no reason why you won't have a positive dating experience online. Just remember to always be alert. Always be on guard. Pray a lot and be sensitive to the leading of the Holy Spirit. But other than that, expect to have fun too. Have the time of your life. It's really not all that bad, I assure you. In fact, if and when you meet the man or woman of your dreams online, all the craziness of the online world will quickly dissipate into thin air.

8

⟨∞⟩

Online Dating
Safety Tips

Although research shows that half of women think online dating sites and apps are not a safe way to meet somebody, there are many steps you can follow to protect yourself. (Anderson et al., 2020) Below are some safety precautions you can take to have an enjoyable experience online. These are just some of the many ways, so make sure you conduct further research. The more security measures you have in place, the better protected you are. The safer you will feel, too. You can never be too careful while dating online or in person.

Note that you may not have to follow all these steps with every person you meet online since not everyone is a fraud. But then again, be prepared to be swamped, especially if you're using a free online dating app. It will be too cumbersome if you have to follow all these with every person you meet. Just learn to weed out the fraudsters, at least the ones you can detect from miles away. There is no need to even give them a minute of your time. That way, you won't have to deal with the frustrations. You get to save time and energy for the deserving ones; at least, that's the goal. You only need to take extra precautions when you're talking to somebody you're truly interested in. Remember, if he (or she) sounds too good to be true, he (or she) probably is, unless you can prove otherwise.

Pray: As a Christian, no weapon is more powerful than your prayers. So, pray unceasingly. Ask for wisdom. Pray for discernment and protection. Pray that the Lord will send His army of angels to protect you from predators and scammers. Recite Psalm 91 daily. Ask for strength to resist temptations. Pray that God will open your eyes if you end up talking to the wrong guy. Pray that the Holy Spirit will lead and guide you every step of the way. Psalm 37:23 says: "The steps of a good man are ordered by the Lord: and he delighteth in his way." God cares about you. He wants to be involved in your life, including your love life. So be sure to include Him. Pray that God will lead you to the right man (or woman) and deliver you from the wrong ones. Be willing to pray that not your will but His be done, and He will graciously keep you from harm. More than that, He will bless you for obeying His will.

Be sensitive to the Holy Spirit: If you're not a Christian and don't understand what this means, let me explain. But before I do that, let me just say that you can become a Christian and have an enjoyable, personal relationship with Jesus Christ. John 3:16 says, "For God so loved the world, that he gave his only begotten Son, that whosoever believeth in him should not perish, but have everlasting life." Regardless of what you may have heard or been told, God loves you. He wants to have a relationship with you. That's why He sent His Son, Jesus Christ, to earth for you. It doesn't matter what you've done in the past. Jesus Christ took away all your past, present, and future sins and bore them on the Cross for you. He took the brunt of God's wrath and punishment (that we deserved) for you so that you didn't have to. Jesus gave His life for you so that you may live and have eternal life with God the Father.

All you have to do is confess that you are a sinner, repent (to turn completely away), and acknowledge that Jesus died on the Cross for you and that He is now seated at the right hand of the Father. Offer your life to Jesus Christ and ask Him to be your Lord and Savior. Ask Him to live inside your heart now and forevermore. Sincerely pray this prayer:

> Lord God, I confess that I am a sinner. I recognize my need for Your forgiveness. Please forgive me for all of my sins. I accept Your death on the Cross as the penalty for my sin and recognize that Your mercy and grace are gifts You offer to me because of Your great love, not based on anything I have done. Please cleanse me and make me Your child. By faith, I receive You, Lord Jesus, into my heart as the Son of God and as the Savior and Lord of my life. From now on, help me to live for You. I surrender control of my life to You. In Jesus' name, I pray. Amen.

If you pray this sincerely, believing in your heart, Jesus will surely come. Revelation 3:20 promises this: "Behold, I stand at the door, and knock: if any man hear my voice, and open the door, I will come in to him, and will sup with him, and he with me." The ball is in your court. Are you going to invite Him? Salvation is now, so I hope you won't wait any longer. There is nothing more that Jesus wants than for you to be reconciled to Father God, for He loves you so much. Or maybe you were once a devout Christian and drifted away; don't hesitate to call on the Father today. Pray Psalm 51 from the depths of your heart, and He will surely come.

Once we give our lives to Christ, we become a new creation and cease living in the flesh. Meaning we are no longer dictated by what we want but by what God wants. We go where He wants us to go and do what He wants us to do. Galatians 5:25 says, "Since we are living by the Spirit, let us follow the Spirit's leading in every part of our lives." Being sensitive to the Holy Spirit takes "practice." Meaning, you will take baby steps before God asks you to take giant leaps. The best way to start is by reading the Bible every day. The Bible is His voice and His Word. How can we know God's will if we don't read the Bible? How can we know that what we're hearing is from the Lord if we don't know what the Bible says? The Bible is the infallible or inerrant Word of God, so it is the ultimate authority. We cannot deviate from what it says.

So, what is it really like to live in the Spirit or to be sensitive to the Holy Spirit in the most practical way? Suppose you meet someone you like, but you just seem restless, uncomfortable, or uneasy. More than likely, that's the Holy Spirit prompting you to stop and let go. To not forge ahead or continue with whatever you're planning to do. Some may even mistake it for someone's gut. If you already feel that the person you're talking to is not who he (or she) says he is, then you're probably right. Don't waste your time convincing yourself that you're wrong. Instead, follow your "instincts." Some try to ignore it and suffer the consequences. Do not be part of the statistics. If something doesn't feel right, it probably isn't. If there's something you're not supposed to do, don't do it. Remember the saying that goes, "Better be safe than sorry."

I once met somebody online who sounded like he might be a good guy. Like the guy who used a 20-year-old photo, this man knew the Bible well, too. He said the right things and answered some of my tough questions. However, something about him didn't seem to add up. But I couldn't seem to pinpoint what it was. I just felt in my heart that something was not right about him. Still, I chose to ignore it, and counted it as me just nitpicking again. We chatted for about two years irregularly, and I was already wondering when he would want to meet. I was in Dubai when we first met online. When I moved to Orlando, he finally brought up the subject of meeting up. I was a little disappointed that the man wasn't willing to fly to Dubai when I was still there. But hey, it is what it is. I agreed, and he asked me for hotel suggestions near my place in Orlando. As we emailed back and forth, I realized he seemingly expected me to stay with him.

I got tired of beating around the bush, so I finally asked him if that was his expectation. He bluntly replied that if he were flying all the way (I already forgot which state he was living in) to Florida to see me, he expected me to stay with him in the hotel. I flatly said no, and that was the last time I talked to him. I was almost livid because I thought he was one of the few good guys I met online. I was obviously wrong. All those talks about him honoring me for preserving myself, about him being chaste, and about how he was waiting for the right woman were all baloney after all. More wasted time (years, in fact), more wasted energy. It was so frustrating. In fact, after this guy, I probably went offline for an extended period as I felt burnt. I thought I'd never go back online again. But thankfully, I did.

My husband, Cantrell, also had an almost similar experience. Years before meeting me online, he considered a girl in Shreveport. She was good-looking, known by people that he knew, and he practically asked older women to introduce him to her. Long story short, there was mutual interest, and they started talking. However, after a few talks on the phone, Cantrell started getting uneasy, restless, sleepless, and uncomfortable about the whole thing. He kept asking God why, but he never got an answer. But when Cantrell finally prayed and asked God if He wanted him to no longer pursue the girl, he would leave it alone. Right after saying that, Cantrell finally had peace. He felt so relieved afterwards and was able to sleep soundly afterwards.

In contrast, when Cantrell met me and was seriously considering marrying me, he was totally at peace. Even I was surprised by the level of peace that I'd never felt before. When we signed the marriage license application in Kissimmee months later, I was so at peace that I felt like I was on cloud nine. I was so happy. Actually, I was so joyful because it was coming from the deepest part of my heart. I've never felt that way before. No, it wasn't euphoria. I just knew that I was doing the right thing by marrying the right man that God had approved for me. There was no fear, not an iota of doubt, and no reservation at all. Hopefully, this gives you an idea of what I mean by being sensitive to the Holy Spirit. The Holy Spirit does speak, but we need to be quiet and sensitive to His voice in order to hear Him.

Google: Since you are talking online, the likelihood of finding more information on someone is almost certain. Unless, of course, the person is an impostor. Make sure you run a Google search on the person you're talking to. It's amazing what you can find on Google nowadays. Most people's details are now public records. You can find people's current home addresses as well as previous addresses. You can find telephone numbers and, most often than not, mobile numbers too. Verify everything the person tells you. You can even find the person's relatives and friends, even ex-spouses. You can find their relatives' obituaries as well as their birthdays. It's incredible how much people share online. You could even find people's passports and driver's licenses. It's insane. But Google sure is a treasure trove of information, if you know how or where to look. So, make sure you take advantage of that.

Reverse Image Search: Make sure you conduct a reverse image search on the person you're talking to. Using Google Image Search helps you determine a photo's origin. This is helpful in finding out whether the person you're talking to is actually the person behind the photo. Or he simply stole somebody else's photo, which happens all the time. To run a reverse image search on Google Image from your computer, upload the photo you want to do a search on. Drop the photo on the search bar and then click search. Follow the trail and comb through the search results. Note that you can only use this on your computer and not your mobile phone. If you are unsatisfied with the result, check other online reverse image search tools like Bing, Yahoo, Pinterest, etc. You can also check out other articles online outlining the top reverse image search tools.

Check his (or her) social media: If there's a person you're interested in, always make a habit of checking out their social media profiles. If they have an online dating account, it's most likely they have a social media account. If not, I would consider that a red flag. I know a lot of military people are not on social media for security reasons. But even if they claim to be in the military (which most scammers say), make sure you check them out on Google. Find their relatives. By checking their relatives' profiles, you should be able to find them on social media. Check their posts. A lot of people like to flaunt their profiles publicly, so you should be able to check their online activities without befriending them.

Don't just settle for Facebook. Look for them on Instagram, YouTube, Pinterest, Twitter, or even LinkedIn. I did the same for my husband. I was a little disappointed that his Facebook account (his only social media account) didn't even have a profile photo. But I did find his friends and siblings, so that gave me some relief. Although I already liked everything he told me, I still wanted to verify the things he said about himself. Finding their social media accounts is not enough. Check how long they've been on Facebook. If they have created their account only recently, that's questionable. Check their posts and their friends. Check his (or her) interactions with friends or social network.

If the account is private, check their profile photos to see who has commented and liked them. You should be able to see how long ago (or how recently) they have created their account. If it's very recent, that goes to show he (or she) only created it for you. More likely than not, he (or she) is an impostor. These are very simple steps you can take, but they are invaluable in finding out whether they're fraudsters or not. Finding Cantrell's family and friends online gave me a much-needed assurance that he really was who he said he was. It wasn't enough to fully assure me, but it was all I needed to make me feel comfortable to meet him in person. So please make sure that you've done your research well. Do not leave any stones unturned. Never take anything for granted. You have to do your own research. Always check, double-check, and triple-check. This is your life we're talking about. You can never take anything for granted.

Check his (or her) church: Another thing you could do, but only a few people bother to follow through with, is to check the church website of the person you're dating. Or even the person's church's social media pages. Before considering marrying someone, make sure that you both share the same doctrine. It may or may not be a deal breaker now, but it might be later. If you're a Baptist and the person you're considering is Pentecostal, you might want to pray more about it. And what better way to learn about your differences in doctrine than by checking out the other person's church?

Before I met my husband, Cantrell, I checked out and listened to some of his pastor's sermons. I knew I was going to move in with him in Shreveport one day if I decided to marry him. So, I had to make sure that I could handle his pastor's sermons. By checking the person's church's website or social media accounts, you might just stumble upon more photos of the person you're talking to as well. Or not. One other way to confirm that he/she is truly a member of a certain church is by checking if he/she has liked that church's social media. That's also another confirmation of the person's identity.

Video chat: If you feel comfortable enough to talk on a video camera after a few days or weeks, hint at it. If the person comes up with excuses for not being able to, then it's time to tell him to take a hike. The person you are talking to is most likely hiding something. Video chatting is the best, fastest, and easiest way to verify that the person you are talking to is the same person behind the profile photo. This is non-negotiable. If they claim to be in the military, please be wary. As I mentioned before, most scammers pretend to be in the military, so they claim they cannot video chat. They cannot speak to you on the phone either, because if they do, you'll realize they're a fraud because of their heavy African or Middle Eastern accent.

And there are various ways you can video chat with someone, so there is no excuse. You can use Facebook Messenger, Skype, WhatsApp, Zoom, FaceTime, Google Chat, WebEx, etc. There are so many options out there, so don't ever give anyone an excuse. Unless, of course, they live in a remote jungle somewhere in Timbuktu or the Amazon. If they say they don't know how to use an app or something and are not willing to try or learn, then drop the person. They are not worth it because they do not think you are worth the effort. Why would you waste your time on somebody like that, anyway? Please don't wait weeks or months. The sooner you cut him (or her) off, the better for you. The longer you keep interacting, the harder it is for you to drop the person. Protect your heart. You deserve the best. A man who's truly into you will do anything to be with you, physically or virtually. Period.

Run a background check: Another invaluable measure to take to protect yourself is to run a background check on a person. Although I didn't run a background check on Cantrell, I did on another man I met online previously. He never admitted it, but I did find something about him that was a red flag. So, try to use whatever available tools are out there, especially if they cost you nothing. There are a few free tools available online, but most cost money. The free tools may not give you much, but sometimes what does come up is enough to help you decide whether to continue talking to a man (or woman) or not. Since Cantrell and I were both Christians, and I listened to him pray often enough to know that he was a mature Christian, I didn't feel the need to run a background check on him. Everything I found about him online corroborated what he told me. But if you feel the need to run a background check on someone, please do. You never know what cans of worms you might unearth. But hopefully, none.

Don't reveal too much info: First of all, never use your real name online. Always use a username that isn't your real name. To my horror, it surprised me to see that some people practically use their full names on their dating profiles. I thought they were exposing themselves unnecessarily and opening up their doors to possible stalkers. It's okay to give your real first name the first time you meet, but never give your full name until you think it's safe. I was always on a first-name basis with the very few men I talked to online. I also let them give me their full name first. I double-checked their Facebook accounts to ensure it was the same person I was talking to. If they were being vague or evasive, I would give them a few more days. But I move on and ditch them if they remain vague. They shouldn't have a problem giving me their full names if they were really interested in me. The only reason they would refuse to give me their full names was if they were hiding something.

Don't ever send money online: Sadly, so many women have fallen prey to unscrupulous scammers online. These are mostly older, lonely women who were divorced or recently lost their husbands. A record $304 million in losses were reported to the FTC in 2020 alone. (Dating or Defrauding?, 2022) Many of these women (and a few men) lost their entire savings and/or retirement funds. Please never send money to someone you have never met in person before. No matter what kinds of overly dramatic stories they tell you, or what kinds of emergencies they are supposedly facing, never send money. If they are not willing to take the risk of meeting you in person, why would you be willing to take the risk of sending them money online? Do not walk away; run away from them as fast as you can. Report them to the dating site's admin and block them. Most admin sites will be more than happy to block them for you. One of the protocols of online dating is to never ask for money, so that's an automatic red flag.

Know the red flags: The Bible commands us to be gentle as a dove but wise as a serpent. The best way to avoid getting conned online is to know the biggest lies scammers tell online. Most often than not, men pretend to be working for the military and claim to be based somewhere in Iraq or overseas.

For safety and security's sake, they refuse to expose their faces, or at least that's what they claim. They insist on communicating with you via email only. Most of these con men are actually based in Nigeria or somewhere else in Africa. Countless women have fallen prey to such con men. You have to outwit them in order to survive in the jungle of scammers.

They will profess their love for you the minute they contact you. I know it's easy to be swayed if you're lonely and vulnerable. Maybe you just lost your husband, and you long for someone's company. Then here comes a seemingly good-looking American man in the military based in Iraq. Next thing you know, you're in a relationship with him without ever meeting him in person. Before you know it, you're "in love" with a phantom somewhere in Iraq or Afghanistan. A few months later, you receive distressing news. He was in an accident and needs money quickly. Can you please send some money? You are his only hope. He is in a dire situation. He's in a remote area. If you don't help him, he will die. No, he will not. It's a scam. I know it sounds harsh, but that's the only way you can protect yourself and your savings. Too many women have already fallen for such traps. You don't want to be the next victim, do you?

Never share sensitive information (including your social security or bank account number): This is probably a no-brainer, but you'll be surprised by how many people let their guards down and share extremely sensitive information in the name of love. No matter what reason the other person gives, don't ever share your social security number, let alone your bank account number. I remember somebody reaching out to me on LinkedIn one day. Yes, LinkedIn, for crying out loud.

Although I found it strange, I thought I'd give the man the benefit of the doubt. Perhaps he wasn't really looking for love and just wanted to connect. This man claimed to be the CEO of some company in Greece. Because I did often get requests from CEOs, VPs, GMs, etc., I thought the man was just one of them.

A few days later, he revealed his true intention. He let me know that he was actually interested in me. I played along, still thinking it was strange. I thought the man was up to something. He quickly sent me photos of himself and his supposed daughter. I was still baffled by the whole thing, but I kept playing along. He only had a few people in his network, but I thought he might be new to LinkedIn, which wasn't strange. A month passed, and his sinister plan came to light. He pretended that he and his associates had come across some oil reserves somewhere in Africa. He needed a favor from me. He needed a bank account to send money to because the amount was way too much. It was at least $50M. Of course, my eyes grew big, and I started laughing.

He sure thought he could fool me. To prove everything was legitimate, he sent me a supposed official letter from Shell showing that they found some oil and that the total amount was the same as the one he told me. The problem was that the alleged official letter from Shell did not have Shell's official logo. Also, the letter was riddled with typos and grammatical errors. Knowing that Shell was such a big company, I thought there was no way somebody who worked in Shell's communication department drafted that letter. I went ahead and finally told the guy that I knew he was a crook and that I was going to complain to Shell about him. The guy pretended to have been hurt and wrote back, saying he understood my hesitation. He never bothered me again. Thank goodness.

As much as you need to be street-savvy to survive in the world, you must also be internet-savvy when surfing the World Wide Web. You need to be aware of the red flags and be ready to shut the door on a person, no matter how good-looking or nice they may seem. Do not follow your emotions; trust your gut. Follow your instincts. Again, if something doesn't feel right, it probably isn't. If you're troubled and have no peace about what the other person wants you to do, be bold to stand up and say no. Be courageous and say no to unscrupulous scammers. Who knows—the more noes they get, the less likely they will try to strike again. In the end, you might be saving countless lives too.

Don't reveal any identifying info: If you have just started talking, there really is no point in going into specifics. Don't give people your home address. Give them your city, not the whole address. If the person tries to grill you, be vague. If the person persists, then shut him (or her) down. Let them know you don't want to share revealing info until you're comfort-able. It's your right to refuse. If anything, it should be a red flag. Tell him to take a hike. The rule of thumb is: don't leave any identifying information—your full name, home ad-dress, where you work, etc. Don't even bother to share any landmarks near where you live or work unless you're already planning to meet.

Meet in a public place: If and when the right time comes to meet, never meet somewhere private. Don't go to his/her house like I did with the guy in Florida that I mentioned in my introduction. You have never met this person before, so no matter how seemingly nice he (or she) is, do NOT meet in a private place. Choose a restaurant that you know will have people in there. It does not have to be a packed restaurant, but at least you know it will not be empty. Otherwise, it defeats the purpose. Or meet in a park, not somewhere isolated but somewhere that has high foot traffic. If you can bring a friend along, please do. An impostor will surely not appreciate you bringing company. But a man with good intentions will respect that about you. But if you decide to go alone, never let your guard down. Always insist on staying in public.

Don't drink a pre-ordered drink: This is a common modus operandi of a serial rapist, so be sure not to drink a pre-ordered drink. A lot of women fall prey to unscrupulous individuals this way. And even if you don't drink someone's pre-ordered drink, always keep an eye on your own drink. Sadly, many date rapes happen because of this too, and way too often. Do not be the next victim. Always be vigilant. Do not get too comfortable at the first, second, or third meeting. If you feel uncomfortable at any point in your meetup, do not feel obligated to stay. You have the right to go whenever you like. No one has the right to pressure you to stay. Come up with an excuse and decline politely.

Drive separately: Before and after meeting up, be sure to drive separately. Never get into his (or her) car, no matter how innocuous he (or she) may seem. No matter what someone promises you. No matter how much they implore you. The probability of you surviving a kidnapping once inside a car is almost second to none. I know these might make you even more terrified, but online dating is really not all that bad if you follow these tips. You have a guardian angel watching over you, so if you are careful and not hasty, you should be okay. If you are picky about the people you talk to, chances are you are going to have a great time talking to the first man (or woman) you decide to meet with.

That is how I met my husband. In my three years of dating online, I only met two other men before my husband. He had never met anyone outside of the dating app before me. He also dated at least two other Christian women in person before me. Yes, that was how picky we both were. In fact, that was one of the first things his pastor told me—that Cantrell was very picky. That's why he was surprised when Cantrell told him he wanted his pastor to meet me. He has never brought someone to church before. Imagine that.

Introduce him (or her) to your family: If and when you find someone online and decide to take it to the next level, be sure to introduce each other to your families. One great indicator of a person's character is how he (or she) treats his (or her) friends and family. So never let an opportunity like that pass. I flew all the way to Shreveport to meet Cantrell's family. Now, mind you, Cantrell's aunt, the family's matriarch, didn't even want me for him initially. She just wanted somebody Black, so when she found out that I wasn't, she wasn't happy.

Despite knowing this, I still flew to Shreveport to meet her. And I was glad I did. Despite Cantrell's aunt's reservations, she fell in love with me at first sight. She refused to let go of my hands for the first 15 minutes while heaping me with compliments throughout. It was almost funny, but it was so worth it meeting Cantrell's family and friends. Everywhere I went, I only heard praise for Cantrell. I even met some of his co-workers and classmates, who were all singing his praises.

Meet each other's pastors: Any godly man or woman would want the blessing of his or her pastors. So, Cantrell and I had agreed earlier on that we would meet each other's pastors before making a life-changing decision. So, when the right time came, Cantrell flew to Orlando to meet my pastor. Once he did that, it was my turn to meet his. After meeting Cantrell's family, I attended Cantrell's church and met with his pastors after the service. This was all the more important to both of us since both our parents were gone. We both looked up to our pastors as our spiritual parents and authorities. Remember, the Bible talks about seeking godly counsel. You should be able to trust your pastors enough to make a good judgement about your date's character. If you don't, maybe you need to find a new church whose pastor you can trust.

This may look like an exhaustive list, but if you follow these safety tips they should ensure that you have a great experience both online and offline. Don't follow these steps, and you will most likely end up with a broken heart. Please do not let that happen to you. You have already waited long enough to make another mistake. Or to go through something difficult again. If you don't want to repeat something, you better do it right the first time. That's what my husband said over and over. He only wanted to get married once, so he was very picky. He wanted to be certain he didn't have to do it twice. So, the choice is yours. At the end of the day, you are responsible for what you do. The way I put it, I would love for you to enjoy the consequences of your actions. Not suffer the consequences of your actions. I hope you see the difference.

9

Top 3 Recommended Online Dating Sites

After covering and addressing the most common questions and concerns people have about online dating, perhaps you're feeling more equipped to dip your toes in the online dating world. But you probably wonder where to start. Like the physical world, the virtual world can seem vast and intimidating. Don't fret; I've got you covered. I wrote this book to help you navigate the ins and outs of online dating. So you do not have to grope and grapple in the dark. One of the first few things you will want to do is try out one or two of the online dating sites that I am about to recommend.

Since my husband and I met and got married five years ago, so many more online dating sites have cropped up. The choices were confusing enough then; they're so much more confusing now. I didn't know where to begin. I didn't know what I should or should not write about myself; I didn't even know whether a dating app was truly a Christian dating site or not. Many of them claimed to be Christians, but the moment you're inside, you realize the majority of the members are not Christians at all. Or simply professing, but not necessarily practicing. It was confusing, daunting, and frustrating all at the same time. So, to help you weed out those that may not be worth your time and money should you decide to go the paid app route, I have listed down and reviewed the dating apps I recommend.

My husband only tried two dating apps, while I tried two or three that I can remember. But I do not want to suggest something I have not personally used. Feel free to explore and experiment though. Then stick with what you're comfortable with. These are just suggestions, and you're more than welcome to follow them or go another route. I can only share what I have personally tested and make a few recommendations based on others' reviews. Since writing this book, a new dating app called Right Stuff has been introduced. It's more geared towards conservatives and people who hold conservative values. If you consider yourself conservative, you might want to try it out too. Again, I never had a chance to check it out, but I do not think there's any harm in trying it. In any case, here are my top three recommended online dating sites, in no particular order:

Christiandatingforfree.com: This is where my husband and I met, so it naturally takes the top spot for us and is our favorite. What we love the most about this site is that it's free, of course! One of my "conditions" with God before

I created an online profile was that I did not want to pay to "find" a husband. I felt God was much bigger than a paid online dating account, so I wanted something free. Besides, I did not know what to expect, so I was not ready to take out my credit card and swipe it for some dating company. Adam and Eve met without having to pay, right?

So, I thought I should meet my Adam without paying for anything. I am not in any way saying it is wrong to pay for an online dating account. I am just sharing that I preferred a free online dating app over a paid one. This was just my preference, nothing more. I am pretty sure there are many benefits to a paid online account. But I cannot really attest to it since I have never tried it. Again, the choice is yours. In fact, most of the people I mentioned who met online and are now married—most of them met on paid dating sites. So, it's really up to you, but my husband and I definitely loved christiandatingforfree.com and highly recommend it. See below to find out my reasons why.

What I liked:
Free for as long as you like
Very easy to use
Very easy to navigate
Quick admin response

What I didn't like:
Has too many unvetted members
Hard to sift through the members
Lots of "frogs" or fraudsters
Image captioning was not user-friendly

eHarmony: eHarmony was probably the most popular dating site in the world among Christians when we were still active online. I know a couple of people who used this and met their spouses on the platform. Both pairs are still together today. However, using this platform is not free. You can try it out for free for seven days, but with a lot of limitations. Check below to note my observations using the free trial version.

What I liked:
Free trial period to just check it out
Complete privacy (nobody can see your photos until you sign up for paid access)
Access to the site's matchmaking program
Most members are seriously looking for a relationship
Trusted Christian dating site
Offers compatibility quiz and dating advice

What I didn't like:
Limited trial period
You can't message your matches
You can't see your matches' photos

Having a paid account will surely allow you to bypass all these restrictions. So don't hesitate to pay if you wish to sign up for complete access.

Match.com: Match is another one of the Christian dating sites that can be really hit or miss. Like eHarmony, it is also a paid online dating site. But it also has a free trial period. Here is my assessment of Match's free trial version. I know of at least one couple who met through the app and got married. As far as I can see, they seem to be happy. So it might be worth checking out too.

What I liked:
Lets you check it out before committing to a monthly bill
You can easily view your potential matches

What I didn't like:
You can view your potential matches, but you cannot message them
You have to pay in order to reach out to your potential match

Based on what I have outlined about these platforms, you should be able to determine whether you want to try any or all of these sites. I would encourage you to try at least two sites so you can compare. No site will be perfect; all of them will have flaws and features that the others won't have. But decide what you want and settle for one or two accounts. That way, you get to have a variety and won't have to deal with the same annoying people. That's what I did. It was almost like a breath of fresh air whenever I went to the other sites because they were not exactly the same.

I have given you the dating sites I recommend. However, I also have a handful of sites I suggest you try to avoid. If you profess to be a Christian, you really shouldn't find yourself on any of these apps. Why? These apps have become widely known as hookup apps:

AdultFriendFinder
Ashley Madison
Bumble
Feeld
Grindr
Tinder
Zoosk

Do your own research and study thoroughly before signing up for any dating app. You can always try a dating app during a trial period, then cancel if you feel uncomfortable. I can guarantee that you will be inundated with requests and proposals. Some sites' members might even send you explicit materials as some users have experienced. (Brickfield & Donahue, 2021) It never happened to me, thankfully, but maybe because I only used those three dating platforms I recommended.

So, please be wise and be very careful. And that's why I encourage you to experiment with more than one platform so you can disable one account if it gets too much to handle. Remember, when it gets too overwhelming and frustrating, feel free to shut down your computer. Walk away for a day or two, weeks, or even months. Take it one day at a time. Be patient, and try to enjoy the journey as much as you can. It's the journey, not the destination, that matters after all.

10

Crafting an Irresistible Online Dating Profile

Before even creating a profile, it is important to determine what you really want in a future spouse. What are your deal breakers? What are you willing to compromise on, and what would you be willing to tolerate? If you go online without knowing these things first, you'll end up chasing after the wind. You'll end up going in circles, moving from one guy (or girl) to another, not being able to say no when you really want to say no upfront. You'll end up entertaining guys that you would never have entertained in the first place. Trust me; I've been there and done that.

Although I was pretty clear about what I was looking for in a man in person, I didn't know what to expect in a man online. I realized that men online could easily project a different persona from what they really are in person. I ended up rejecting more men than I had anticipated because many of them pretended to be the kind of men I was looking for at first. Without discernment, they could have easily fooled me. But I also realized that if I had been upfront and firm about my likes and dislikes, I would not have had to go through all those "frogs." If you don't want anyone to waste your time, be firm about your standards. Try to see through a man's (or woman's) profile before interacting with them. If you have any doubts, you are most likely right. Many might not agree, but I do believe that a man's (or woman's) profile should say enough about the kind of man (or woman) he (or she) is.

If you think he (or she) may not be a good fit based on what you've seen so far, then most likely, he (or she) isn't. A lot of my mistakes were caused by ignoring that little prompting from the Holy Spirit that the man I was looking at was not good for me. Were you ever told to not judge a book by its cover? Well, when dating online, you should do exactly the opposite—judge him (or her) by his (or her) profile! Instead of listening to the Holy Spirit, I listened to that old adage. I often thought maybe I was reading his profile wrong. Maybe I was being judgmental. Maybe I was being critical. I should give him the benefit of the doubt. Maybe it's not what I think. But if I had listened to the Holy Spirit, I could have avoided being annoyed or disappointed countless times.

So, if you want to spare yourself from a similar emotional roller coaster, please make a list of your standards. Be specific. Do not be shy about it. You should know yourself well enough to know what you really want. But be honest. Don't look for a perfect partner when you yourself aren't perfect. Make sure you're not looking for a housemaid or a servant but a life partner. Do not expect something from somebody that you yourself would not be willing to give or do. In other words, do not expect your future spouse to be someone you're not willing to become yourself. If you want someone who's a perfect 10, then you better make sure you are a perfect 10 yourself. I hope you get the point.

Once you've written out your list, make sure you present it to God. Make sure that your list aligns with the Word of God and is not just a bunch of unrealistic expectations. Once you've made certain that your list is practical, wise, and biblical, promise yourself that you will not waver from your list. That no matter how long the wait takes, you will stick to it. Commit to it before God. A man who really knows what he wants won't have to test drive every car he sees in the parking lot. Meaning, a man won't have to go out on a date with every potential girl he meets. The same goes for women. It always baffles me why a woman goes out with almost every single man that approaches her. This clearly stems from the woman's insecurity and lack of sense of identity.

Please remember who you are. You are a child of God. You deserve the best, and you are also the best for someone. You should be able to discern whether a person is right for you or not. My husband often told people he had met enough women to know what he didn't want, so when he met me, he instantly knew I was the right woman for him. Be precise, decisive, and purposeful. Do not jump from one relationship to another while tearing a part of your heart each time you break up with someone. Preserve yourself for the man (or woman) of your dreams. And if you have already compromised or lost it, do not be discouraged. Do not feel condemned. God is able to make you whole and make you new. Just be willing to give Him all the pieces of your heart. It's amazing what He can do with them if you let Him.

Next, determine your intention, or shall I say your level of intention? Are you looking for a casual date or a future partner in life? Before creating our online dating profiles, my now-husband and I were clear on one thing: We weren't looking for a casual date. We were seriously looking for a future partner in life. We were so serious that we wouldn't even entertain people we knew we would never be interested in. We just never believed casual dating would do anyone any good. We both believed in being intentional about what we did, especially about dating. A lot of men (or women) make this common mistake. They are seriously looking for a spouse but end up entertaining those who clearly say they are only looking for a casual date.

Even in person, you see a lot of frustrated women (and men) in casual relationships. The women expect their men to propose despite knowing that their men made it clear from the very beginning that they weren't looking for a serious relationship. The same thing goes for men. They want to propose to the women they are with, but the women made it clear at the onset that they were not ready to get serious. This creates so much friction, frustration, and heartache. So, make sure you know what you want and stay with what you want before you even start dating, online or offline.

The good thing about online dating is that you can easily determine who is looking for a serious relationship or not. That helps greatly in weeding out who you'd want to talk to. The same goes for you. If you're just curious, some online dating apps also have this kind of status option. But if you decide to get serious, you can easily switch to the appropriate status. Don't ever bank on the idea of being able to change the mind of the man (or woman) you want to be with. Please do not do this if you do not want your hopes dashed. It is also not fair to pressure a man (or woman) to get serious with you if they have been clear about their intentions right from the start.

Determine how motivated you are. The level of your success in finding a life partner is contingent upon your motivation level. As I mentioned in a previous chapter, if you're just toying with the idea, online dating may not be for you. I have a couple of friends who were deeply motivated to find a partner in life and casually tried online dating. But both gave up after a few glitches because they were obviously not that motivated about finding someone online. Perhaps they were waiting for signs from heaven—thunder and lightning, maybe? Perhaps they were waiting for their future life partner to fall on their laps or knock on their doors. Determine your level of motivation and decide that you will do everything you can to find a godly man (or woman) with the grace of God and the guidance of the Holy Spirit.

Once you've factored these all in and are happy with your answers, begin to work on your online profile. If you're looking for casual dating only, then be sure to select that. If you're serious, then be sure you select "seriously looking." Most online dating apps have pre-selected questions to help you create your profile. Be honest. You have to be as transparent online as you are in person. Remember, online dating is not much different from in-person dating. Online dating is really more of a misnomer. It should be called an online meeting. You don't necessarily date online; you simply meet online but actually date in person. Or at least that's how it should be. I know, I know. A lot of people end up falling in love without even meeting in person. That's a scammer's modus operandi: hook you in, then leave you high and dry. But ideally, you are supposed to meet online, meet in person, and then date physically, not virtually, which leads me to the next tip.

Meet online but date in person. I know that sometimes distance can be an enormous factor. But I would really discourage having a relationship with someone you have not met in person yet. Make this one of the criteria in your profile. Do not be coy about it. If a man is truly intentional and sincere about you, they will cross oceans and climb mountains to see you. I know some will make empty promises. As I mentioned in a previous chapter, I once dated a man in person, and all he did was make empty promises to see me later. When I left Orlando and went to Cebu in the Philippines, he promised to visit me in Cebu, but he never came. When I moved to Manila, he promised he was going to visit me there, but he never did. When I moved back to Dubai, he promised he was going to visit me there but never did. It was a series of empty promises, and I have only myself to blame for believing he was sincere somehow. When I went back to Orlando, I didn't even bother to meet up with him again.

But in most cases, a man who's truly into you will find a way to see you no matter what, just like Cantrell did. He flew a handful of times to Orlando just to see me. Unless, of course, you live thousands of miles from each other. But if you meet somebody online from another city, you really shouldn't wait too long to meet in person. A week or two of chatting on the platform should be enough to help you decide whether it is worth exploring the idea of meeting in person shortly. Or if you should stop talking to the person altogether. Don't take it to extremes, either. I knew of someone who was based in Dubai and met somebody online who was living in the USA. They never met in person but dated online for about a year. When they finally met in person, they both flew to the Philippines (where the woman was from) not to meet, but to get married.

I firmly believe this was an unwise way to marry someone. I would never recommend it to anyone. I am not saying this is morally wrong. It is not my place to declare it right or wrong. I am simply saying this is an unwise and unsafe way to meet and get married. Imagine the unnecessary pressure if the man or woman turned out to be so different in person. Imagine if the man had sinister plans and already knew where you lived. Or imagine the big disappointment if it doesn't work out at all. Thankfully, in this instance, the man seemed to be genuine. It is imperative that you meet in person first before deciding to get married. Chatting on camera is way different from dating in person. You need to get to know each other in person. Online chatting should never supersede dating in person.

Again, "online dating" is really more like "online meeting," but dating should be done in person. I remember meeting an American guy online way back in college. It was still the days of Yahoo Messenger or Yahoo Group Chats. I had not yet finished college, and a common friend was chatting with the man initially. My friend eventually introduced me to the American, and we ended up chatting with each other more. We weren't "dating" at all. We were just two people on different continents, curious about each other's cultures. At the time, I had never been outside of my country, and he'd never been outside of his country, either. Neither of us had many previous interactions with foreigners, so we were both curious. We talked mostly about our Christian beliefs. The more we talked, the more we realized how much we had in common.

We decided to try video chat a few months later. I gasped at the first sight of the man. He looked handsome, albeit boyish. He was only one year older than I was. I was 20; he was 21 at the time. He had gleaming green eyes that reminded me of a cat's eyes, red lips, and reddish hair. Like me, he was also waiting for the right woman. He worked for the United States Air Force and had not found anyone special yet. I secretly wished then that I would be that special person. He never told me what he did, but he said it had something to do with computers. I had secretly wished to marry a pilot, but since he worked for the Air Force, I thought that would do too. We were just "online friends," though, so I tried to control my then fast-beating heart.

Fast forward two years, and the guy and I were still "just friends." Meanwhile, I tossed back and forth almost every night, asking God if He would turn the man's heart towards me. We seemed perfect for each other. Not long after, I left the Philippines to work in Dubai. I was afraid of wasting more of my time on the American, so a few months after I arrived in Dubai, I asked God one last time if the American was the one for me or not. I was ready for a yes or no answer.

Either way, I would have been okay. I was ready to let go and move on. I felt in my heart that God told me no, and that was it. I decided to forget my feelings for the man, and I was surprisingly at peace. There was no inner struggle at all. I was simply at peace; I didn't have any regrets either. I was surprised, but the fact that I was at peace made me feel that I heard right.

I went about my life and proceeded to forget the American. We still chatted on Yahoo Messenger occasionally, but the attraction was not there anymore. I also got busy with work—a new city, new people, and new friends. I thought it was time to start a new life in Dubai. But seven months after I heard God say no, the American suddenly revealed his feelings for me. He said he had been waiting for the right time, but there was just never a right time. So, he finally said he's been interested in me for a long time. He was not looking for a casual date. He was interested in me, and he was in it for the long haul—marriage, that is. I was almost shocked. I could not believe he was finally saying what I had been waiting to hear for the past years.

But I knew that I heard God say no about this man. And it was already too late. I had no more feelings for him. So, with as much grace and courage as I could muster, I politely said no. Even if it meant saying no to somebody I had admired for years. I had no prospects either but I stood firm, even if it meant saying no to what seemed like a good catch. Even if it meant not knowing whether a new quality guy would ever come my way again or not. I was determined to obey God. I trusted God's plan for me and knew He had a bigger reason beyond my understanding. Everything suddenly went quiet.

That was the last time I heard from the American, at least for the next two years.

Life went on, and I got busier with church activities. The American soon became a faint memory. Two years after I rejected the American, he contacted me out of the blue on Yahoo Messenger. I was caught by surprise. I thought he was a goner. I never once expected him to reach out to me again. I knew my rejection wasn't a small thing for him. He was back to being himself and acted as if nothing had happened. Fast forward six years, and I bid my last goodbye to Dubai and traveled to the USA. Since the American was in Florida, I thought we owed ourselves a chance to see each other in person. After all, he's been a faithful online friend all these years. He readily agreed. We agreed to meet at a Kentucky Fried Chicken in Orlando, not too far from where my sister lived at the time.

I recognized the American instantly, even as he got out of his car in the parking lot. He has obviously aged. Gone was the boyish look that I used to admire. To be fair, it had been over ten years since I first saw him on video. The man walking towards me looked so different from that guy. The man in front of me had thinning hair, was almost bald, and had pockmarks on his face. He wore a pair of brown corduroy pants and a faded brown collared shirt. He staggered a bit, as if he were carrying the weight of the world on his shoulders. Suddenly, it dawned on me. In a way I could not explain, I finally understood why God said no to the American. Just by looking at him from a distance, I could see that he wasn't my type at all. As he got closer and opened his mouth, my conclusion was even more magnified. I just knew that even if we tried, it would not have lasted.

I thanked God silently for saying no to me when I prayed about the man, and for the grace to have heard Him right. It was a big learning moment for me. It only reinforced to me the importance of trusting God, even when what He says does not make sense. I thought the guy was perfect for me, but God sure was right. And many times in our lives, what God tells us to say or do will make no sense. Perhaps you are in a situation right now where it makes no sense. But if God is telling you no, trust Him. Obey Him. You may not understand it now, but one day you might. It truly is true what they say: "Father knows best." I prefer to say that "Father God knows best." Add in the fact that God knows us way better than we know ourselves. There's no better judge of who's best for us than God. He sure is the greatest matchmaker. I just have to look at my husband and myself. So, please be sure to meet or date in person before going any further with someone you encounter online.

Create a striking and honest summary about yourself. Be as specific as possible; don't be generic. As the saying goes, you attract what you project. If you want to be shady, then guess what? You will attract shady men (or women). If you project yourself as a casual dater, you will attract casual daters. If you really want somebody serious, then make your profile look and sound serious. I always wanted someone who had never been married before. But in the early stages of my online dating experience, I flip-flopped about this. Whenever I felt that I would never find anybody who had never been married before, I'd flip and start talking to men who were divorced or widowed. But then, the thought of dealing with their teenage kids always scared me. I often turned my account on and off until I finally got tired of dilly-dallying.

After three years of flip-flopping online, I finally decided to be single-minded. I decided not to be swayed by my emotions anymore and trust God to send me the right man. I determined beforehand that purity or celibacy was very important to me, and so I made that a priority. Instead of just describing it in the inner section of my profile, where it was buried, I practically posted it on my summary so anybody could see it right away. This was the first thing anyone saw when they checked out my profile. I thought it would either deter men who are no longer pure or are not celibate. Or it will pique the curiosity of those who were or have the same mindset. I wasn't going to fool around with those who professed to be Christians but were comfortable sleeping around. I was wrong. It did not deter them, but their numbers drastically dropped. So, I can safely say that having your standard plastered on your profile really helps.

Talk about yourself. What are your likes and dislikes? Do you like to travel? Talk about it. Do you like to cook? Mention it. Do you hate spiders or snakes? Don't be afraid to share that. The point is to make your profile look interesting and hopefully attract someone with whom you share something in common. Talk about the things that matter to you. The goal is to draw someone in who shares the same values as you do. Be honest and transparent. But also leave some for the other person to discover. Do not bare it all, as they say.

Describe the kind of person you would like to meet. Talk about your passions—music, theater, sports, missions, etc.

You want to meet someone who shares the same interests as you. Do not be afraid to talk about your fears too, but again, in moderation. You do not want to scare the right kind of men unnecessarily, either. For example, if you've had a traumatic childhood, you do not want to share that at the outset. Wait for the right time. No need to spill all in your profile, or in the early stages of your interaction.

When it comes to photos, make sure that you are not sharing revealing photos. If you do, then be sure to expect perverts to be attracted to your profile. Do not share photos of you in bikinis or swimsuits. Why would you? I know modesty is such a contentious topic (and I really don't understand why). But if you really want someone who will love you for you, why try to attract someone with your physical beauty? Would you not rather be admired for your intrinsic qualities than your outward appearance? If you are well traveled, show photos of you at readily recognizable landmarks. A fellow traveler will surely catch that.

If you're into gardening, share photos of you in your garden. A fellow botanical enthusiast will surely be drawn to your profile. And please, only use photos that are at least three years old. If anything, you should use a current photo. That's also helping the other person set the right expectations. Share photos of you in a natural setting and share photos of you all dolled up. Show them your many facets so they have an idea of how you look in various settings and realize how interesting you are.

These are just some of the many ideas on how to create a truly eye-catching profile. Check out other women's (or men's) profiles. Even men's profiles will surely give you great ideas about what they are looking for. And if you meet their criteria, then that will definitely help you create your own profile too. I'm not saying that you need to create a profile that matches exactly what they're looking for. You have to be yourself, but keep in mind what a potential mate might want to see in your profile that can help him weed out other women. Think about what attracted you to a man's (or woman's) profile. Most likely, it's something you would want to put on your profile, too, if it resonates with you.

11

121 Questions to Ask Him (Or Her)

So, let's say you've created your online profile and you've met an interesting guy (or gal). Now you're ready to talk on video or even just on the phone. But you're terrified of making a blunder. What if you say the wrong things or ask the wrong questions? What if you make a fool of yourself by not knowing what to say? What if you are feeling shy and intimidated? What if you lose your tongue suddenly? No worries; I've got you. It is quite normal to be a nervous wreck and tongue-tied just before your very first video call or phone call.

I remember my first video chat like it happened yesterday. I was scared of the same things as you probably are, but the guy I was emailing with seemed interesting. I went ahead anyway and as it turned out, I really didn't have much to worry about. If you are a natural talker in person, I can assure you that the conversation will flow naturally virtually too. But just in case you're still unsure of what to say or where to begin, I've outlined the following list of questions to help you kick off your chitchat.

Avoid asking yes or no questions; that's a surefire way of keeping the exchange short and boring. You're not accomplishing the goal of getting to know the person behind the screen or on the other end of the line. You might never have to ask all these questions, but you probably will find many of them quite helpful. Feel free to add what you think might be missing. Based on their answers, always try to follow up with another question. Don't sound like you're reading a script.

Make it sound as natural as possible by closely listening to what the other person is saying. Be sure to react and not stick to your script or list of questions. Remember, you are talking to someone you might decide to marry one day. So you'll want to know the person as much as possible. You also want to know that what he (or she) says is true. Look them in the eye. Watch their body language. Do you think they are being honest? Are they being sincere? Or are they just saying what they think you want to hear?

It is pertinent that you look for red flags in their answers. As you go through this list, you will notice that some are self-explanatory. Others are not, while some are repeated for emphasis. I have added more insights on what kinds of answers to look for. What kinds of questions to ask in reply to their answers. I also personally share my other conversations with Cantrell as best I can remember them. I share what my concerns were as we continued our talks and how we both overcame them. Remember, the person you are talking to, if he (or she) is sincere, has as many questions and concerns as you do. After all, love is a two-way street.

It is also like a job interview. You are (or you should be) eager to know about the hiring manager and the company as much as he (or she) wants to know about you. So be prepared to ask questions, but also be ready to provide answers. Ask God for discernment so you can readily tell whether the man (or woman) is telling the truth or not. When you're just starting, keep your conversations or topics light. As you progress and talk more often, you can shift gears and move to a more serious discussion.

Conversation Starters

How did you come to know Christ? If he (or she) is being vague, make sure you ask more questions. Ask them to be specific. *When did it happen? Where did it happen? How did it happen?* If the person on the other end cannot give you specifics, then most likely that person is lying. Giving one's life to Christ is a life-changing experience that one can never forget. So, if the person cannot remember the year when he (or she) gave his (or her) life to Christ, you should really question the authenticity of the person you are talking to. If they cannot remember what happened or what prompted them to give their lives to Christ, they are most likely just telling you what you want to hear, not necessarily the truth.

What do you do? Tell me more about your work. Keep a wary eye on anyone who claims to be an American, works for the military, and is based overseas. As I mentioned in a previous chapter, scammers pretending to be working for the military have victimized too many women already. You do not want to become a statistic. If they insist they are, ditch the guy and move on to the next person. And let the "military" person know you will be happy to talk to them when they are back in their hometown. Or when they are ready to tell you more about themselves.

What is your favorite Bible verse or chapter, and why?

Who is your favorite Bible character apart from Jesus? Why?

If you could choose, during which biblical time or age would you like to live?

What is your favorite movie?

What was the last book you read (apart from the Bible)?

What brought you to the dating site? What has your experience on the dating site been like? Or other dating sites? What do you like about this dating site? How long have you been on this site?

What do you like to do in your free time? How do you like to spend your free time?

What kind of church do you attend? Is it non-denominational, Baptist, Pentecostal, etc.? Again, try to prod for more details. This is how you would know if the person is a real believer or not. Just to warn you again, just because the person knows the Bible well and can quote Bible verses, it does not necessarily mean he (or she) is a Christian. Or that he (or she) walks the talk. Christianity is a lifestyle, not something you do on Sundays or on occasion only.

Can you tell me more about your church? What do you love about your church? If they truly belong to the church they claim to be a member of, then they should be quick to let you know. See if he (or she) really loves his (or her) church. If they are active, they should be able to share specific church activities that they love to do. They can tell you more about it in detail.

Do you like to travel? Have you traveled outside the United States (or wherever)?

Do you generally like meeting new people? Why?

Are you interested in different cultures? Why are you interested in my culture (if applicable)?

What are you studying (if applicable)?

Who is your favorite preacher, pastor, or minister? Why?

What do you like about your city? If I were to visit your city, what sights would you recommend? This is another litmus test to see if the person you are talking to actually lives in the city they claim to live in, or if they are actually from there. Don't ask for something that can be easily Googled; ask for things that only locals would know.

Do you have any claims to fame? Have you ever been featured in a magazine, won awards, etc.? If so, ask for more details if they are willing to share.

What is your favorite food? Favorite ice cream flavor?

What is your favorite board game?

Are you an indoor or outdoor person? Ask the person to expound.

If you were stranded on an island, what would you bring?

What is your favorite childhood memory?

What is your favorite sports team and why?

What's on your bucket list?

What do you like about your job?

What was your dream job as a child?

Are you a morning person or a night owl?

Are you an introvert or an extrovert?

As you continue to chat or talk, you will surely come up with more interesting and light questions. Or you can always fire back the same question he (or she) asks you. The main goal is to get to know each other better. The other person has just as much right to ask you questions, so be prepared to give your own answers. Be honest and sincere, even if you feel the other person is not. And if they are being a jerk, politely excuse yourself, and then hang up. You deserve the best, so do not feel bad about ending a call abruptly if you do not feel right about the person on the other end. Or if the other person is not giving you the respect and attention you deserve.

Prodding Questions

Do not be afraid to dig deeper as you start to talk more often. Feel free to ask any or all of the following questions. Remember, the more you know about him (or her), the easier it is to make wise and godly decisions about the next step or stage of your relationship or friendship. No one apart from you can tell the perfect time to ask these questions. But you should be able to gauge when you are both comfortable with each other. Some of these questions can be asked right at the very beginning. I fired some of these hard questions at Cantrell at the onset myself.

I was so tired of beating around the bush with previous men that by the time Cantrell popped up online, I wanted to get rid of him as soon as I could. I thought if he were a true Christian, he would be able to handle it. If not, he will buckle and scurry away like a scared dog with his tail between his

FINDING TRUE LOVE THROUGH ONLINE DATING ~ III

legs. Thankfully, Cantrell turned out to be a strong man of God. Never be afraid to ask the questions that bother you. You have a right to know, with discretion, though.

Are you active at church? Ask what kinds of activities he (or she) is involved in. If the answer is vague, then ask about the people working at the church. That will let you know if the person is actually active or not. He (or she) should know the people in charge of certain activities and who is involved. Remember to check the person's church website and social media accounts. That is, if the person tells you the actual name of his (or her) church.

Can you tell me more about your family (or kids)? Gauge how deep or shallow your previous conversations have been. If you think you both are ready for a deeper or more meaningful conversation, try to find out about his (or her) family. If not, you can ask this much later. Make sure you ask about his (or her) parents. Try to see what his (or her) relationship is like with them. If it's not a good one, try to find out why. See if he (or she) is just being rebellious. Or maybe he (or she) had abusive parents. Don't rush to judgement.

Be gracious and understanding, but also be discerning with their response. As you must know, how a man (or woman) treats his (or her) parents is a big determining factor of a man's character. It's also a telltale sign of how he (or she) will treat you. I'm not saying no one is irredeemable or incapable of changing. But if the person you're talking to is a true Christian, he (or she) will not badmouth or be condescending to his (or her) parents. Does the person have some unforgiveness issues? Listen and discern.

What do you think of missions? This is a question you need to ask if you want to find out if your calling is compatible with his (or hers). It is imperative that you know your own calling before you even ask this question, though. Or even if you are not into missions, at least find out what he (or she) thinks of missions. *Have you ever been involved in missions? Tell me more about it.* Remember that just because a person is active at church or involved in missions, it is not a surefire sign that he (or she) is a good Christian. I have met men who went to church more often than I did but still turned out to be jerks. I had a friend who met someone online who supposedly led a team of missionaries to Africa during the course of their interaction. He, too, turned out to be a clown and left my friend hanging.

What are you looking for in a man (or woman)? Listen to the answers clearly. Is he (or she) highlighting physical attributes (ephemeral) or internal attributes (enduring)? A person who places so much emphasis on physical qualities is a shallow man (or woman). Proverbs 31:30 teaches us: "Favour is deceitful, and beauty is vain: but a woman that feareth the Lord, she shall be praised." This Bible verse is both a warning and a hint. Do not go after qualities that quickly fade away. Look for qualities that will last.

What are you looking for in a future partner in life? This is almost similar to the previous question. But if the answer to the previous question is vague, you can reemphasize by asking it another way.

Are you here to date casually or are you seriously looking? You can ask this if you want to make sure that they are actually serious. Some do indicate that they are seriously looking, even though that is far from their intention.

Have you met up physically with anyone from here? What was your experience like? Where do you normally meet? What do you like to do when you meet someone in person? Look for red flags. Listen for alarm bells. Does the person you are talking to like to meet in private or public places? Ask for specific details like locations or names of the park or restaurants. The internet is a treasure trove of information. If the person is honest, you can always Google the places later. See for yourself if it is the kind of place you would want to meet in person for the first time. If it's mostly isolated areas, then you already know what to do. Don't just stop talking; block that person.

Have you had any serious relationships with anyone from an online dating site before? Ask why the relationship ended or failed. Check to see if he (or she) blames the other person completely. It takes two to tango, so if the person you're talking to refuses to take responsibility for his (or her) own mistakes, then he (or she) is most likely irresponsible. Determine who is the common denominator in his (or her) failed relationships. That's a good indicator if the person you're talking to is worth keeping or not.

How would you describe your walk with Jesus right now?

Do you believe in dreams, visions, and prophecies? Why or why not? This may or may not matter to you, depending on your denomination. If you don't believe in these, then skip it. But if you do, make sure you are both firm believers. Cantrell was Pentecostal, and I was a professing evangelical when we met. Although I became a Christian in a Pentecostal church, I quickly stifled the Holy Spirit when I joined an evangelical church in Dubai so I could blend in. This was something

I deeply regretted. It may not be a deal breaker, but it is important to tackle this at the onset.

What do you think about speaking in tongues?

Do you believe in fasting? Is the difference in theology a deal-breaker for you?

Do you like children? How many would you like, if any?

What are your spiritual gifts?

Do you have a mentor or someone you run to for personal or spiritual advice? Do you recognize a mentorship's importance?

What is your take on abortion?

What do you believe about the importance of going to church? Or church membership?

What do you think about drinking? Smoking?

What do you believe about homosexuality? Do you support ordaining transgender people as leaders in their congregations? Make sure you are on the same page on this issue.

If someone gave you $1 million, what would you do with it? The person's response should give you a glimpse of their money mindset.

Are you a shopper or window shopper?

Is money a curse or a gift?

What makes you tick? What makes you happy?

How close are you to your family?

What's your ideal date?

What are you most passionate about?

How important are holidays to you?

Questions to Ask Before Committing to a Relationship or Getting Engaged

What is your love language? Ask whether it's words of

affirmation, quality time, physical touch, acts of service, or receiving gifts. Ask them to explain what their love language looks like and/or what their expectations are.

How far would you go? How far is too far? Believe it or not, I never thought this question was even necessary to ask among Christians. But ever since I went online, I've learned so much more about people's dating behaviors than I ever cared to know. Apparently, some dating couples who call themselves Christians are totally okay with fondling each other (heavy petting) as long as they don't go all the way. Whatever happened to holiness and purity? Doesn't the Bible urge us to keep the marriage bed sacred?

If you value purity, as I did, then you definitely need to ask this question. Make sure you dig deep, because men who are simply out to get you in bed will give you vague answers. Or they will give you the answer you want to hear. But in reality, they don't really care. In the end, their true intentions will be revealed, but hopefully, it won't be too late for you. The last thing I want is for you to fall for someone who pretends to be godly but tricks you into doing something you will regret for the rest of your life. I pray you will never fall prey to a wolf in sheep's clothing. Sadly, there are far too many of them in churches nowadays, both virtually and physically.

What do you think about purity and holiness?

What is your opinion on celibacy? Make sure the person understands the difference between purity and celibacy.

What are your boundaries in a relationship?

What do you think of professing Christians living together before getting married?

What are your deal breakers? What are your non-negotiables?

What does a healthy relationship look like to you? There should be mutual respect, not just for each other but for each other's opinions and boundaries. There should be open communication, realistic expectations, and a willingness to compromise on both sides. But be sure to determine that the person is not just telling you what you want to hear. Ask for specific ways he (or she) will keep communication open, develop mutual respect, etc.

What do you think is God's call for your life?

Why do you think God would want us to be together?

What can you tell me about your last relationship/marriage, if any? You want to know why the relationship fell apart and see if the person solely blames the other party. Or is he (or she) taking responsibility, at least partly? *What did you learn from your previous relationship/marriage, if any? What would you change in your last relationship?*

How do you spend time with God? What do you do during your devotional? How often do you do your devotional?

Are you an investor, saver, big spender, debtor, or shopper? This is a very interesting question to ask not only to find out each other's money personality type, but each other's take on money and/or spending. Define each personality type as another fun way to discuss it.

Do you have a budget?

How important is alone time to you?

Are you a spiritual or religious person? Please explain.

Questions to Ask Before Getting Married

Let's talk about sex: *How often?* Expectations need to be laid out at the very beginning. This often causes a rift between married couples, so be sure you both have laid your cards on the table before saying, "I do." Make sure you have realistic expectations. Be honest about what is acceptable to you in the marriage bed and what is not; that is, your willingness to experiment or not. It is important to discuss this beforehand, so there are no surprises. The last thing you want is to end up crying on your wedding night (or later in your marriage) because your groom (or bride) is asking you to do something you were not expecting or comfortable with.

Money matters: It's common knowledge that money is the number one reason couples divorce. (Palmer, 2022) So make sure you talk about your financial obligations before you exchange marriage vows. *Have you ever declared bankruptcy?* If yes, ask the person to explain. *Do you have debts that I need to know about?* If yes, ask what the person's plans are to tackle them. *How do you think that would play out in our relationship?* This question is about managing expectations. Some people, unfortunately, go into relationships expecting the other party to shoulder or take over their debt. Both parties have to be very clear and honest. If you know you cannot pay off a debt on your own, then be honest about it. It is better to discuss this beforehand before it blows up in your face.

Before we got married, Cantrell revealed to me that he had some business debts. To be honest, I didn't know what to make of it. I always believed that when you marry someone, you marry into their wealth as well as their debt, if any. I was prepared either way. Thankfully, Cantrell did not expect me to help him pay off his debts; he was just informing me. On the other hand, I knew a wonderful lady who got engaged to someone who didn't know she had some personal debts.

Sadly, the guy called off the engagement after learning about her debt. I do not know if there was a communication breakdown between them. But I honestly believe a debt shouldn't deter you from marrying someone you truly love. As long as you manage expectations and work out a plan, there shouldn't be any reason why you cannot forge ahead. As for the two of us, we managed to stave off Cantrell's business debt.

Who will manage bank accounts? Do we both have access to all accounts, or will just one person manage accounts? This is another sensitive but necessary topic. Some married couples only have one party with access to all accounts. I personally do not think this is fair. What if that party dies? What happens to the accounts? An even bigger question to address is: What happens to the remaining spouse if they cannot access the accounts when they need it the most? But if the other person is fine with it, then it should not be a problem. Again, there has to be a mutual agreement and not a monopoly. Remember that marriage is a partnership, so if you are truly going to be partners, you should have equal rights and access. My husband and I have access to all accounts, so if anything happens to either of us, neither of us will be left hanging.

How many children? This is a very important question, especially if you have always wanted to have children. You have to make sure that the person you are marrying is totally okay with having children. I heard of a Christian woman who married a man she loved. Sadly, two years after getting married, the husband suddenly declared that he did not want to bring children into this world because of all its miseries. It naturally devastated the wife. All she has ever wanted was to become a mother. I think it was unfair that the husband was not quite honest with her from the very beginning. Granted, I do not know if that was always his plan, or if it really was a sudden change of mind. Either way, it left his wife with very little or no option at all. You wouldn't want to be in this lady's shoes especially if you badly want to have a child someday. Honesty is always the best policy. *How will we discipline our children? Who will be the disciplinarian? What are your limitations in terms of discipline? Spanking or no spanking?*

Are we renting or buying a house? Some are totally okay with renting, while others are not. What if you and the person you plan to marry have opposing views regarding renting or homeownership? You have to be very honest about this, as it can cause so much strain in a marriage. If there was one thing that Cantrell and I had a huge discussion on after getting married, it was this very same issue. Cantrell was comfortable renting while waiting for the market to go down. I was not. After three years of renting, I desperately wanted my own home. For two and a half years, I bugged Cantrell about owning a home. I knew we were ready financially, but the market was not. But I reached a point where I got tired of paying rent and not seeing any returns for it. So, we finally agreed and got our home. Be sure to lay down your cards because you might wear each other out if you are not on the same page. Know that the issue of renting or owning is a common bone of contention among married couples.

Are we paying cash for the wedding or borrowing money? I have always heard it said that you should never start your marriage with a huge debt. If you decide to borrow money just to get married, then be prepared to pay it off sooner rather than later. There is nothing wrong with having a civil wedding, either. Both are pleasing to God and acceptable to men. What is important is that you are legally married and living in a way that is God-glorifying.

Cantrell and I opted to go for a civil wedding because, quite frankly, that was all we could afford. We will get married at church eventually, but for now, I know we are both grateful that we chose not to get buried in debt. So, decide what is more important to you—a grand wedding with debt or a simple wedding without debt. Unless, of course, you have rich parents or benefactors. Personally, I think it is wiser to invest in a grand home where you'll spend the rest of your life than in a grand wedding that you'll enjoy for just one day. But it's your call, not mine.

Theology: *Which church are we going to commit to (mine or yours)? Which preachers are we going to follow?* These were the hardest questions that Cantrell and I had to ask each other before getting married. We could see that we were really perfect for each other, but when it came to theology, we had concerns. I grew up Pentecostal but soon abjured my beliefs in speaking in tongues, dreams, visions, and prophecies when I joined an evangelical church in Dubai. Some of the church's members mocked anyone who followed so-called "prosperity gospel preachers."

But Cantrell was a huge fan of Pastor Joel Osteen and Ms. Joyce Meyer, two of the most prominent and unjustly labeled "false preachers." Cantrell also spoke in tongues and believed in dreams, visions, and prophecy. I was torn between jumping on his bandwagon and receiving the mockery of some of my old churchmates. Or stay in my backyard, lose someone as valuable as Cantrell, and keep my almost nonexistent friends by then. In the end, the choice was easy. I chose Cantrell, of course. Not only did I gain a super amazing husband, but my passion for the same theology was also quickly reignited. In the process, my faith really grew too. I was also so thankful for Cantrell's pastor in Shreveport and the valuable teachings he preached weekly.

I also started listening to Pastor Joel and Ms. Joyce again. Both have been a great encouragement to me for the past few years. I realize now that what I believed about Pastor Joel and Ms. Joyce before was something I heard from others. I have not heard their so-called "false teachings" myself, so I thought I should give them a chance. And I am so glad I did. I could relate so much to Ms. Joyce and all the childhood trauma she experienced. I understand myself better, as does my husband. With Ms. Joyce's practical insights and down-to-earth transparency, my husband can understand me better and relate to me in a deeper way. Make sure that the person you're marrying is not going to clash with you in terms of your doctrine. It could lead to an endless cycle of arguments you wouldn't want to get caught up in.

Tithes and offerings: This is another testy topic and a common cause of friction among married Christian couples. *Do you believe in tithing and/or giving?* Make sure you ask the person you're considering to marry about his (or her) thoughts on tithing. I personally know of couples whose wives believe in tithing but the husbands do not, and vice versa. This is more common than you think. Either way, it is a difficult situation to be in, especially if you believe in the power of giving. I seriously believe that the key to prosperity is generosity, which includes faithfully giving tithes and offerings. I have seen it firsthand in our marriage.

The more we sowed and gave away, the more we were blessed. We have personally received miraculous or unexpected checks in the mail worth tens of thousands of dollars. We have received raises and bonuses and all sorts of tangible favors from the Lord. All of this began when we started giving faithfully. And we make sure that we not only give our tithes but that we also give more than 10% of our tithes as offerings. I saw how truly blessed are those who faithfully give. But the ones who refuse to give 10% of their income live from paycheck to paycheck.

Unfortunately, unless they understand the law of sowing and reaping, they will most likely remain in this cycle. Meanwhile, it's fascinating to watch Proverbs 11:24 play out in our lives regularly: "One gives freely, yet grows all the richer; another withholds what he should give, and only suffers want." As I mentioned before, the number one cause of divorce in America is money. If you choose to marry someone who does not believe in tithing, know that you could be planning to fail. Even if you do not end up in divorce, you will surely struggle financially, emotionally, and mentally. But why choose to struggle when you can thrive under the blessings of God by choosing the right partner with the right beliefs?

Leadership or headship in marriage: *What is your understanding of leadership and submission in the Bible? Are we equal in our roles, or are we equal in everything?* This is quite a common point of contention in marriage. Either the wife wants to wear the pants, or the husband is too domineering or controlling. Or the husband is weak that he simply submits to his wife and agrees to everything she says. I have seen far too many marriages with wives acting as heads of the household than I can remember. What kind of marriage are you hoping for? A biblical marriage or a marriage based on the world view? Your own answer will determine what kind of man (or woman) you will marry. Whatever you decide, be prepared to either enjoy it or suffer the consequences of it.

Unfortunately, there are many pastors out there who are very gentle and loving in public but very abusive to their wives and children behind closed doors. There are also wives out there who are submissive to their husbands in public but emasculate their husbands in private. You have to decide what kind of wife (or husband) you want to be. Not as the world thinks, but as God thinks. Ask yourself, "Is the kind of marriage I want God-glorifying or not?" What am I basing my ideals on—the Bible, the inerrant Word of God, or what the world dictates? Your personal answers to these questions will reveal your true intentions, whether they are aligned with God's plans or man's.

What does it mean to put your partner's needs above your own?
What does it mean to become one flesh?
Will we have family devotions? How often?
Will we pray together as a couple? As a family?
How will we make decisions as a couple when we disagree?
What does submission in marriage look like to you?
What do you believe is the purpose of marriage?
What does it mean to put your partner's needs above your own?
What does it mean to become one flesh?
Have you been intimate with anyone in the past? This is not meant to condemn anyone but it's also important to

be honest about past sexual relationships before exchanging wedding vows.

Have you ever been forced into a sexual relationship in the past? This is a very important question to ask if you feel that the person you're about to marry had a traumatic past that he/she needs to unburden. It's crucial to know what you are getting yourself into so you can be better prepared.

Are you attracted to anyone of the same sex? If you have any doubts at all, and you really want to know that the person you are considering to marry is a man (or woman), you have to be prepared to ask this difficult but important question.

This may or may not be an exhaustive list for you, but if you do need more thought-provoking, soul-searching, and truly insightful questions, please check out Dr. John Piper's list of questions to ask when preparing for marriage. (Piper, 2009) The questions really helped Cantrell and I get to know each other before we decided to get married. It was almost like having a premarital counseling session on our own. But if and whenever you can, we highly recommend that you go through premarital counseling. It sure is a great way to determine if you are compatible with each other or not.

There is a saying that goes, "You can't see the picture if you are in the frame." Seek godly counsel, as the Bible states. Let others help you see things that you may not see. I have seen couples break up during counseling after realizing that they are not compatible, or when the other person has not been forthright. I have also seen couples complete their counseling even more sure of each other. There is nothing to lose but a lot to gain when you invest in premarital counseling.

12

〰️

Top 10 Things to do Together Virtually or in Person

Online or offline dating need not be boring. There are many things you can do together to break the ice initially and keep the conversation going. By following the questions in the preceding chapter, you should be able to maintain a decent level of conversation. But here are other ways to better enjoy your virtual or face-to-face interactions with each other. Apply some or all of these to keep your exchange more exciting and going.

Bible reading: There can be no better way of getting to know each other than reading the Bible together. Decide on a book you would like to walk through together, virtually or physically. Read each chapter together beforehand, or you can read it while you are chatting or meeting in person. Ask what each of you thinks about what the writer is actually saying in each verse. Focus on the context, not just on the verse per se. A lot of misinterpretations stem from an unwise way of unpacking the Bible. So, learn together to unpack it verse by verse, chapter by chapter. Dig deep and ask each other where the writer is coming from and what the author is actually saying. Not what you believe the writer is saying. Discuss how you can apply the lessons practically. Relate it to your life—whether it's relationships, work, family, or life in general.

Praying together: If you truly desire to honor God in your current or future relationship, there is nothing more powerful than praying together. If you are just getting to know each other, as you progress, make sure that you close each chat or meet up with a prayer. Any true godly man would want a woman who knows how to pray, and vice versa. If anything, this is what will make or break your budding relationship. If the person shies away from prayer, then I suggest running away from that person. A man who claims to be a Christian but refuses to pray is no godly man. A truly godly person would jump at the opportunity.

Hearing a man (or woman) pray is also a great determining factor of a man's spiritual maturity. A man is to be the head and pastor of the household, so if a man does not know how to pray, he is not right for you. Perhaps he should cultivate his relationship with Jesus first before pursuing a relationship with the opposite sex. A woman keeps the home together, so if she refuses to learn how to pray, she is also not worthy of your time. Move on to the next person. You want somebody who truly loves God and fears God.

Book reading: You can do this together, both virtually and physically. Decide on a book that you both would like to read. Check who your favorite Christian authors are, and if you find common ground, decide on the book. If you're doing it virtually, you can read it beforehand and discuss your key takeaways from the book. Or you can read it together virtually, chapter by chapter. Ask what you love about the book—your likes and dislikes. Ask how you can apply the insights in real life, especially in relationships.

Visiting a park/having a picnic: If you have determined that both of you love the outdoors, there is nothing better than exploring a park or sharing a picnic. Visit a lake nearby. Take boat rides together if they're being offered. Or even ride a bike together in the park. Spend as much time with each other while setting clear physical boundaries. And whatever you decide to do, always make sure that you stay visible in public. Do not go somewhere remote. Play it safe, always.

Movie watching: If you both like movies, this is something you can do together physically or even virtually. Just share what channels you are on and what time, and you can discuss it while watching. That is not always an ideal thing, but you can also talk in between commercials. You can also watch each other's reactions virtually. This is another way of getting to know each other's quirks and mannerisms. Or you can watch it separately and discuss your likes and dislikes when you meet virtually. Share what you liked best and what you disliked most, and why. Highlight your best and worst parts. Talk about how you can relate it to your current situation, your work life, or your life in general. Emphasize how you can relate the movie to godliness and/or Christianity.

The goal is not just to have something to discuss but to always point each other to Christ, encourage one another, and spur each other on. If you are doing this in person, I suggest doing this much later in your relationship, not at the onset. I highly recommend not doing this at your first meetup. Also, make sure you are in an exclusive or official relationship. So try not to rush to do this. If a man insists on doing this with you much sooner, run away from him. A truly godly man would honor your boundaries and respect you for them, not do the opposite.

Connecting over coffee: This is the least stressful way to meet in person. Remember, you do not need to have breakfast, lunch, or dinner on your first date. Just grab a cup of coffee, say, for one hour. No pressure. Within minutes, you can decide whether to stay longer or cut it short. If you enjoy each other's company in person, you can decide later if you want to meet up again.

Playing a game: Whether tennis, golf, badminton, or horseback riding, go and do something fun, outside and in the open. Find out what sports you both like and discuss a place to hang out. This is yet another fantastic way of getting to know a person. You get to see them in their best and worst lights. A truly competitive person will unravel on the field. They cannot help but show their frustrations when they are losing. Or you can truly see their character when they are winning. So, encourage whoever you are talking to, to do something fun and exciting with you. If he (or she) really wants to get to know you, they will love the opportunity to spend time with you this way. But if geographical boundaries prevent you, then talk about your favorite games and decide on what you two can play virtually together.

Watching a concert: One other way to get to know each other is by watching a concert together. You can do this virtually or physically. If you are both into symphonies and operas, many orchestras offer free shows occasionally. Sign up for their newsletter so you can stay up-to-date with their promotions. Be sure to share the link with each other. You can watch it together, virtually, or separately. Discuss the highlights of the show and what you loved. Talk about your favorite instruments or your favorite parts of the performance. Share about your latest experiences and why you love such shows.

If you plan to do this together, make sure you are watching a Christian concert. Although you are meeting in a public place, there is still a lot that can go wrong. So be wise about when and where you meet. Be careful about what kind of concert you decide to go to together. I suggest doing this in person after you have already gauged the other person a little better. Please do not do this physically in the early stages of your relationship.

Visiting each other's church: During the latter stage of your relationship, you will have to decide to visit each other's church. Eventually, both of you will have to choose whose church you are going to attend. So, what's a better way of finding out than by visiting each other's church? Then you can decide. For some, this is not even a factor to consider if you live in separate states or countries. The woman usually moves to where the man lives. But some situations may not be so straightforward, so it is definitely up for discussion. But if you live in the same state or city, one of you will have to give up his (or her) church.

I heard of a couple whose marriage almost fell apart because the woman decided later that she didn't want to go to the man's church anymore. In the end, the man gave in and decided to attend the church his wife preferred. I wish it had stopped there, but the husband started bashing the church he used to attend. Why not just attend his new church and keep quiet about his old church? I'm sure he had his reasons for following his wife, but he failed his previous pastors by badmouthing them. He also lost a valued friend in the end.

So, if you want to avoid such conflicts, be very careful about things you might take for granted. Get to know them deeply so there will be no surprises later on. Remember, too, that deciding which church to commit to is not about either of you. It is about what God wants you to do together and where He wants you to be. So always check with Father God. Father God knows best, remember?

Attending a Bible study: After visiting each other's church, check out each other's Bible study groups if possible. It is better to see early on if it is a group you will comfortably blend into or if it's something you will struggle to adapt to. It's better to be honest now than regret it later. Do not go to a Bible study, pretend you love it, and then decide after marriage that you do not want to be a part of it at all. That results in contention and bad fallout. So, determine early on what you both want so no one is subject to frustration or disappointment. These are just some ideas to help you foster a healthy relationship. There are numerous other approaches you can follow and apply.

Hang out with older married couples from church. Ask their permission to visit and observe them in their own home. Some couples would love and welcome the idea so be sure to take advantage of the opportunity. They will appreciate your willingness to learn from them. Dine with them if that's an option. Ask numerous questions. Babysit children from your church. Learn and prepare yourselves together. That's the key to knowing what might await you once you get married. It will also help you better understand each other; you will get to see each other's strengths and weaknesses. You get to witness each other under pressure. You will surely get a better idea of whether you're compatible with each other or not.

13

How I Found My Own True Love Online

This chapter should be titled "How My Own True Love Found Me Online," because that's what really happened. But since this is what attracted you to this book, we'll keep it as is. Well, we've finally reached your most-awaited chapter. You've probably skipped over some chapters so that you can get to the best part, this one. No problem. But I encourage you to go back and read the other chapters you skipped because I want you to be prepared once you start navigating the ins and outs of the online dating world. That said, my husband and I met on the online dating platform Christian Dating for Free.

We were both drawn to it because it was free. Like me, Cantrell wanted something that didn't require him to pay a single dime. Since I began this book with me driving on I-4 in Orlando, I will start this chapter from where I left off, in Orlando, Florida.

"Why, God, why? Why is it so difficult? Why is it so hard to find a true man of God?"

I was crying again for the nth time in my bedroom, in the 3-bedroom townhouse I was sharing with two younger girls. As I shared in my introduction, I had just "dumped" a man I had met with a couple of times previously.

We met online a month before and met in person a week later. He sounded so nice at first. He was very active at church, which was one of my indicators that he was a real Christian, or so I thought. He knew a lot of Bible verses, which I found very impressive. I have always longed for somebody I could serve God with, so I thought I had finally found the right kind of man.

But the first time I met him in person, I was disappointed to realize that he looked so different from his picture online. Even though I video chatted with him for a week before deciding to meet in person, I was still taken aback. He looked so unkempt and rugged in person. He was so handsome and youthful in his photos that I expected someone more good-looking. I tried to brush off my disappointment and decided to enjoy the place anyway.

From the restaurant where we met in Lakeland, a city in Florida I had never seen or heard of before, we decided to drive separately to Hollis Garden, located a few miles away. Being the adventurer that I was, I was more than happy to explore and see the garden. And I was glad I went because I thoroughly enjoyed the garden with its flowers and grand porticoes. Although my date looked rough, he turned out to be a fun companion after all. He was a gentleman and was sweet throughout the afternoon.

Before heading back to Orlando, we decided to meet the following weekend in another place—Tarpon Springs, apparently famed for its Greek heritage. It was also the man's hometown, so I thought I could kill two birds with one stone. The man asked me to meet him at his place. Although I will never recommend doing this, I felt comfortable enough to agree. I knew his church and address and left a digital trail for friends to know my whereabouts. We had been talking for about a month already, and I knew it was time to get to know each other a little better. I drove back to Orlando that day, thinking that dating a man online wasn't so scary after all. Little did I know how our next meetup would pan out.

We continued video chatting throughout the week prior to our second date. In the process, the guy finally confided in me that he was a slob. So that explained it, I thought. He also apologized for not dressing up before meeting me for the first time. He said he wanted to show me who he really was and did not want to be a hypocrite. Fair enough. He also wanted to show me his house so that I could judge for myself if I could live with somebody like him. So I went, and again, I was glad that I did although I highly discourage you from doing this.

The man was not kidding. His house, which looked more like a nicer-sized trailer, was covered in dust, grime, and litter. He was not a hoarder, but candy wrappers, old newspapers, socks, pants, etc., littered the floor of his living room. The litter stretched all the way to the kitchen and beyond. Almost all corners of the house were covered with litter. I immediately decided there was no way I was going to live in the man's house. I knew that he was too old to change his habits. I was afraid he would make me his personal maid. I didn't want to be rude and tried to stay for a few more minutes. Although deep inside, I wanted to run as far away as possible.

I had to remind myself that he was a "brother" in Christ, and I had to treat him with respect just the same. Thankfully, he offered to show me the old town shortly after. We went for lunch in a packed pub near the dock. After exploring the town for an hour or so, we ended our adventure atop a rickety observation tower facing the Gulf of Mexico. The sight was so dramatic, and although I was not sure I wanted to see the man again, I could say that it was almost romantic until I heard the next words on his lips.

"Well, since it's almost sunset, why don't you stay the night? That's how my daughter was formed, after all." I was shocked. All this time, the man had been a perfect gentleman, a seemingly godly man. All this time, I thought the man remembered and respected my boundaries. I tried to ignore his remark, but I could not shake it. I remembered that when we were at his house, he also hinted about me spending the night. I thought he was suggesting that I stay in a hotel, but hearing him say what was truly on his mind, I almost threw up.

His suggestions were revolting and insulting at the same time. I realized it was time to go, and I bid the man a final goodbye. I cried all the way back to Orlando, feeling so defeated and deflated. After meeting so many frogs (what I call false male Christians) online, I thought I had finally found a prince. But this man was actually a frog pretending to be a prince all along. All the years of frustration suddenly welled up in me.

I cried to God, as I had done a thousand times before. "Why God? Why? Why is true love so hard to find? Why is it so difficult to find a good man?" I wondered what else I could have done to make sure that the person I was talking to was genuine. I have probably already met hundreds of men online. I thought I was already an expert on weeding out fraudsters. But there I was—duped again by another man for the third time in a row. In my three years of online dating, I have only taken three men seriously, and all three turned out to be frauds. All three of them had the same goal in mind—to get me in bed with them.

How could they claim to fear and love God when they are no different from the men of this world? They all seemed to know the Bible well, were active at church, and spoke Christian lingo. But they all didn't believe in keeping oneself pure before marriage. Later that night, as I lay in bed crying, I told God that I was done with dating or courtship. Period. I was sick and tired of the emotional roller coaster and the mental anguish. Three years of casually looking online and a lifetime of waiting offline.

I felt like I had reached the end of my rope. If I had to be single for the rest of my life, so be it. I told God I was done trying unless God Himself brought the right kind of man to my doorstep, literally or figuratively. Oddly enough, the following day, I got a notification on my email that I had received a message from somebody new on the online dating site. I tried to ignore it. I thought to myself that I was not going through that emotional high again only to be disappointed later on.

But I was reminded of my prayer the night before. What if God took me seriously and He did bring the right man to my "doorstep"? But what if God did not, and this was just another fraudster? I wrestled with myself and vacillated for a few hours, but I could not shake the thought that he might be a man from God. Curiosity got the best of me, and later that afternoon, I hopped on to christiandatingforfree.com once again. I quickly read the man's profile, and it looked very interesting. Everything he said about himself resonated with me.

Cantrell (which turned out to be his name as you must already know), was a high school teacher based in Shreveport. "Shreveport? Where is that?" I wondered. I quickly Googled Shreveport and found out that it was a city in Louisiana that I had never heard of before. I've heard of Baton Rouge and New Orleans, but Shreveport? Never. And why would a man in Louisiana be interested in me when he can see I am based in Florida? Very interesting indeed. But other than that, everything I saw initially looked good. I could see that we had so much in common, especially in terms of our beliefs.

He only had a few photos. I thought he looked younger in his profile photo, but at least I knew it wasn't 20 years old. Although I liked what I saw, I had to stop and double-check myself. Have I not gone down this rabbit hole before? Am I willing to go through all the disappointments again? But something in me told me to give the man a chance. And so I did. Reminded of the disappointments from the previous day, I decided to give Cantrell a hard time. I thought there was only one way of knowing right away if he was legitimate or not.

I thought if I asked him hard questions, I would surely scare him away. So that's exactly what I did. But Cantrell quickly proved me wrong. The first question I fired at Cantrell was about purity. I asked him if he truly believed in purity since his profile suggested that. I have seen it in a few other men's profiles before, so I was skeptical. He responded the next day, saying he did and explained why. He also wrote back that he, too, was preserving himself for marriage. I could not believe it. He was the first man I have interacted with online who was actually doing it, not just saying it or talking about it.

But still, I remained apprehensive. I wondered if he, like the other guys I met, was just telling me something I wanted to hear. But then, before I was able to reply, Cantrell sent me another message, correcting what he had previously emailed. He clarified that by purity, he meant chastity. He had done things in the past like worldly guys did, but ever since he gave his life to Christ, he has preserved or made himself chaste for the past 22 years. He was praying that his future wife was doing the same. My jaw dropped. I wondered if he was being honest. I mean, why would he correct himself if he wasn't being real?

The fact that he was willing to admit his past mistakes said volumes about his character. But I was determined to continue investigating before I gave him the benefit of the doubt. I continued firing hard questions at him, but each of his replies impressed me even more. Cantrell also asked me hard questions with each of his responses. We exchanged long emails for about a week before he dropped another bomb. He told me he was considering coming to Florida to check me out in person. To use his own words, he thought he'd heard and seen enough to decide I was worth investigating.

Florida was his favorite holiday destination, so his visit would also be twofold. Although I was excited to hear that he was planning to visit, I was surprised. I knew we were enjoying our exchanges, but I thought it was too soon. I had no idea he was already that interested in me. Or at least that's what he said. I wondered if I should believe him. He seemed so genuine, but I knew I needed to tread lightly. I'd been disappointed before, so I didn't want to be disappointed again.

I also remembered that Cantrell was not the first man to tell me he wanted to visit me. I realized that dishonest men like to drop that hint to lure women in. Or to keep them excited and interested, although they really have no intentions of following through. So again, I kept my heart in check and tried not to get excited. I acted casually and told him I thought it was cool that he was coming. But Cantrell proved himself different yet again. Before I could react further, Cantrell explained that he was not planning to come right then. He would have to wait a month or so until his classes were over.

I heaved a sigh of relief. Not only because I knew I wasn't ready to meet another man in person, but it also gave me a sense of assurance that he really was genuine about his intentions. I shelved the information and thought I would wait until he gave me specific details about his itinerary before I would believe him. And he did. The next few weeks came and went in a blur. Cantrell and I quickly moved from the dating site to emails, from emails to phone calls, and from phone calls to video/Skype calls. The more I talked to Cantrell, the more I believed he was legit.

He was unlike any of the men I have met online or offline before. He seemed to love and fear the Lord genuinely. He told me about his prison ministry and how he has been doing it faithfully for the past 11 years. He was ministering to about 150 inmates at the time, which was bigger than the members of some of the churches I knew. He was practically a pastor in his own right. But I never once heard him brag about his ministry. He seemed so down to earth—almost too humble to a fault. He shared with me his faith journey and how he came to know the Lord. I was beginning to like him more and more while struggling to keep my heart in check.

We talked more about our standards, and we both laid down our cards. We both did not hold back. We shared our non-negotiables and our aspirations. On our second week of video chats, I finally asked him to close us in prayer. The truth is, I was just testing him. Everything I had seen and heard so far was good. But did the man really know how to pray? He hadn't proven it yet. I thought that would be a deal-breaker if he didn't know how. But I was in for another big surprise. The first time I heard Cantrell pray, the door to my heart popped open unexpectedly. I was suddenly drawn to Cantrell spiritually, something I was not counting on happening so soon.

It is safe to say that this was the first time I truly saw who Cantrell really was in the Lord. I fell in love with his spirit that night. I almost wanted to be like him. I loved how he prayed; it gave me a glimpse of his beautiful heart. That was how I always wanted to fall in love. I wanted to fall for a man's spirit and character first, and he with mine. Even in the past, I was turned off by a few other men's true characters. Some women get easily blinded by looks or titles, but not me. Looks, titles, and possessions are fleeting, but not a man's character. It's almost "eternal." So, I was really excited to see that Cantrell was genuine.

The ensuing four weeks of video and phone calls every night really drew us together spiritually. We grew so at ease with each other that it felt like we had been friends for years. I was more than ready for him when he finally came to Orlando. We first met in person at Cantrell's hotel's parking lot in Altamonte, Florida. But I faced a hiccup right away. I was not impressed with Cantrell's physical appearance. He was okay-looking but not exactly what I was expecting, physically, at least.

Don't get me wrong. I didn't think Cantrell was ugly or anything. I just was not physically attracted to him, at least not at our first meeting. He was wearing an orange and white checked dress shirt and a pair of brown dress pants. "He dressed up, at least, unlike the last guy I dated," I thought. I really appreciated that he took the time to look good for me. It made me feel like I was important to him and that he valued me. I thought he was a tad too formal for the occasion, but I really liked that he tried to make a good first impression.

I could also see that he knew how to carry himself. "At the very least, he wouldn't need help choosing his clothes like some men," I thought. He was confident without being arrogant. He wasn't shy, but he wasn't aggressive either. We proceeded to the Outback restaurant near his hotel for our first official date. The food was great, but the conversation turned out to be even better. At one point during dinner,

Cantrell leaned forward and reached for my hands. I thought that was a bold move. I knew we really felt comfortable with each other, but I was not sure if we were both ready for that. I guess he was too excited to have found me. He could not control himself.

When I asked him about it after we got married, he did not even remember that he held my hand for a brief moment. He just remembered having a really great time with me and enjoying my presence. He asked me about financial management and how I was preparing for the future. I told him I would love to, but I did not really have any assets to manage. Let alone any finances to manage. I wondered then if he had more money than he was willing to let on.

But we were not officially on yet, so I did not pry. We moved to Cranes Roost Park nearby. After watching the park's small fountain dance to the music, we moved closer to the lake. As we leaned on the rails, Cantrell reached for my hair and parted it from my face as a sudden gust of wind blew. Again, I thought Cantrell was being bold. We were not official yet, so I was keenly aware of every physical touch he made. I knew it was innocent, but I was still a little wary after being disappointed by other guys.

After five minutes, I motioned for us to go back to the bench we were sitting on moments ago. When we went back, that was when we realized that Cantrell had actually left his phone and car key on the bench. We were surprised to find they were still there. Thank God no one else had sat on that bench! Our guardian angels were obviously watching over us. We've laughed and joked about it since then. His usual excuse—that I distracted him! Later that night, before I went to bed, Cantrell called to ask what he needed to wear the following day, Sunday, to church.

Being a Black man, he was used to Blacks dressing to the nines when going to church. Since he did not know my church's dress code, he wanted to check with me first. I told him that some dress up, but most wear casual clothes. He thought he would dress it up, and I encouraged him to do so, although I wasn't sure if I should have. I wondered what dressing up meant for him, as if he hadn't already dressed up earlier. Well, at least I get to see him in his Sunday best, I thought. I mentally prepared to dress up a bit too, just in case. I was not going to look underdressed next to him.

That night, I was still mulling over the fact that I did not find Cantrell physically attractive. I believed that he was a great man of God. I knew that his heart was genuine and that he was a man of good character. Should I ignore the physical part? I knew you were not supposed to marry a man (or woman) to whom you were not physically attracted. But you were not supposed to marry a man (or woman) for physical attraction alone, either. I was in a bind. I wasn't really sure if I needed to bring it up to God. Or should I just let everything flow and fall into place? I just kind of brushed it off and expected God to know what was on my mind, so I didn't even bother to articulate it in prayer.

I just thought that if Cantrell was right for me, surely even the physical part would eventually work out. I just needed to trust God and the process, as I had in the past. And God heard my unuttered prayer yet again. The following day, I reached the hotel before Cantrell did. Minutes later, Cantrell called me, saying he was in the parking lot. I decided to wait in the lobby. As I turned and saw Cantrell walk through the glass doors, I gasped. I suddenly exclaimed, "Wow!" before I could stop myself.

Walking through the glass doors was a dashing African-American man in his white dress shirt, black dress pants, and silver and black bow tie. I couldn't believe Cantrell's transformation. From a not-so-attractive man to a sharp-looking hunk! I was swooning. I almost wanted to run to his arms and claim him as mine. At that moment, I practically fell head over heels for Cantrell. I was so proud that he was dating me, and not some other girl. I was so thrilled that we were together. I realized it wasn't because Cantrell was not good-looking when I first met him the day before. I just didn't like what he was wearing then.

I was smiling from ear to ear as I walked with Cantrell towards the sanctuary. But then I remembered I hadn't had a chance to warn my pastor about Cantrell. I wished I had been more upfront with my pastor about Cantrell and me dating. That was the whole point of Cantrell's presence at church—to meet my pastor. But since I didn't tell my pastor beforehand, I couldn't get him to talk to Cantrell more intentionally. I managed to introduce them, but people were always thronging my pastor, so they didn't have much time to talk. Please learn from this mistake. Warn your pastor beforehand so he can set aside time to really talk to the man (or woman) you're dating. I was glad they met but wished they had more time to talk. I only had myself to blame for that.

Cantrell's presence at church was just another test of his sincerity towards me. A dishonest man would have come up with excuses not to meet with my pastor. So, this is another factor that you need to consider. To cut a long story short, Cantrell asked me to be formally his a few days later, just before he left for Shreveport. Oh, yes, he didn't waste any time. I did check with my pastor the next Sunday, and he said he did not feel or see any red flags about Cantrell. He also added that he had peace about Cantrell, although he, too, wished that I had told him that we were dating so he could have talked to him more. Once Cantrell flew back to Shreveport, we continued our nightly video chats. This time, we were more persistent and intentional with our questions.

Since we were both clear that our end goal was marriage, we followed John Piper's list of questions when preparing for marriage. I have covered a similar list of questions in this book, but please feel free to check John Piper's list on the Desiring God website. (Piper, 2009) The questions were tough, but they really helped us determine if Cantrell and I were truly a good fit for each other. Since we did not have a formal premarital counseling, it was like we had our own during those video or Skype calls. We always prayed before we concluded our talks for the night. We would usually video chat for about an hour, but occasionally we talked a little longer. There were times I felt the presence of the Lord come down during our prayer times. They were sweet and precious moments that I truly cherished.

During those prayer times, I felt that I had really found the man I wanted to marry. For the first time in my life, I felt so at peace. There were no what-ifs, at least not at the time. Cantrell was the first man I felt so spiritually intertwined with. It felt like we fit each other like a glove. Soon it was my turn to visit Cantrell's family and meet his pastor. I was excited at first. But as we went through the list of questions further, fear started creeping in. I started doubting whether Cantrell's pastor might like me or not. As I checked Cantrell's church's website and Facebook page, I thought Cantrell's pastor sounded so spiritual. What if, for some reason, he ended up not liking me? What if he ends up claiming the Lord told him I was not the one for Cantrell? What would Cantrell do? When I asked Cantrell one night during our video chat, Cantrell said he would have to cancel our plans.

I almost crumbled. I was afraid Cantrell's pastor might turn out to be like some "pastors" who decide who's right or not for their members. My heart was gripped with fear. What if Cantrell decides to break up with me after flying all the way to Shreveport? What should I do? Should I go ahead and take the risk? As I had done in the past, I wanted to sabotage my relationship with Cantrell. I wanted to end it before it went any further. I wanted to say goodbye to him before I got hurt.

Negative thoughts raced through my head. I could already see myself facing a dark and foreboding future. I had already imagined the worst likely scenarios before I even met Cantrell's pastor. But as I pondered all these in my mind, Cantrell did not seem perturbed. He just kept staring at me on camera. I expected him to back out and tell me to just cancel our plans since I was having doubts. Instead, he just kept staring at me silently, waiting for me to say something. When I saw him quietly waiting on me, I finally realized the foolishness of my thoughts and fears. Nothing had happened yet, and yet there I was, already imagining the worst of the worst. I haven't even met Cantrell's pastor yet, but I was already thinking the worst of him.

What if I turned out to be wrong? Was I willing to risk losing Cantrell because of my baseless fears? What if Cantrell's pastor approves of me after all? I would have lost such a quality man like Cantrell for nothing. I had a choice to make at that moment. Listen to all the negativity and baseless fears in my head. Or listen to what I know to be true—that Cantrell was a great man of God, and I might never find anyone else as amazing. I remembered that God does not give us the spirit of fear but of power, love, and a sound mind. All of my fears were based on my imagination.

I was simply making up excuses not to go ahead with the relationship. They were clearly coming from the devil and not from the Lord. I also realized that if I didn't go, I would live the rest of my life in regret. It's better to risk being disapproved by Cantrell's pastor than live in regret, not knowing for sure. I could not imagine living with so many what-ifs. Was I willing to wait another lifetime for someone like him? I finally broke the deafening silence and told Cantrell I was going through with my plans to fly to Shreveport. He simply said, "Good."

All my fears suddenly went away. I instantly regained my faith in us and believed that everything was going to be alright. And I was right. All my fears turned out to be baseless. The devil was clearly bent on stealing my future and killing my hope. Cantrell's pastors turned out to be so warm and welcoming. They seemingly liked what they saw in me. We didn't even have to ask them for their blessing. They simply blessed us and prayed for us right there and then. It was a real pleasure meeting them. Cantrell's pastor even bragged about Cantrell in front of the congregation, saying that so many of his members get married before introducing him to their spouses. Only after the marriages have started crumbling do they remember to seek him out for help or advice.

Whereas, with Cantrell, he flew me all the way from Florida to meet his pastor. Even Cantrell's aunt, who initially didn't approve of me for Cantrell, fell in love with me at first sight. She held on to me for fifteen minutes as she gazed up at me from her wheelchair and kept telling me I was beautiful. I got to meet not only Cantrell's immediate family and his pastors but also his relatives, schoolmates, and workmates. Everywhere we went in Shreveport, we bumped into people that Cantrell knew. Everybody was congratulatory and always had amazing things to say about Cantrell.

I couldn't help but marvel at the goodness of God. I went to Shreveport not knowing what kind of reception I was going to have. Yet all my concerns turned out to be pointless, as everybody was seemingly accepting and approving. I fell in love with Cantrell even more and saw how privileged I was to be with him. My trip turned out to be even more special and worthwhile when Cantrell asked me to marry him at the American Rose Garden. I've always dreamt of being proposed to in a rose garden, so that was another dream come true. It took a long time, but it finally happened.

After spending four beautiful days in Shreveport and meeting so many people, I was ready to go back to Orlando to prepare for our wedding. We drove for four hours back to Houston, where I caught my plane back to Orlando. It was a bittersweet goodbye, albeit necessary. I could not wait to be reunited with my love. On the plane, I could not help but cringe at the thought that I almost broke up with Cantrell the week prior. I was teary-eyed and grateful that God sustained me through it all. If I were still the same person I was, always sabotaging any chance at a good relationship, I would not be engaged. The thought alone made me shudder.

I was so grateful that I finally broke through. That I was truly in a relationship with someone deserving of me. In fact, Cantrell was so good to me that there were times I wondered whether I deserved him. I had never met anybody so esteemed by everybody around him. It was so fascinating that someone like that was actually mine. It was one thing for one's family to speak highly of a family member, but when it's the co-workers and high school classmates, etc., that's a whole new level. Cantrell was almost too good to be true, but he sure was oh-so-true.

Cantrell and I got married a month later. You might think that was too quick or too soon. By then, we had only known each other for about four months. Well, remember that both of us had already waited our lifetimes. So, we thought, why should we wait any longer? We were both sure of each other. We had both waited long enough to know what we needed or wanted. We were both of age, not too young to be naïve. Just before our wedding, Cantrell's pastor announced our nuptials to the congregation. He also mentioned that Cantrell was marrying a woman who had never known a man before, while many have fooled around.

Cantrell's pastor also shared the fact that Cantrell himself had preserved himself for 22 years. I knew that without telling us explicitly, Cantrell's pastor was proud of us, and we were so blessed to know that. Both my sisters and their families joined us at our civil wedding in Kissimmee, Florida, which made it even more precious. My pastor and his family's presence at our wedding made it even more special. I felt so blessed to have had these people at our wedding. At the small wedding reception, one of my sisters insisted we take photos because the wedding was 40 years in the making. I couldn't help but smile.

For our honeymoon, Cantrell and I stayed at the most beautiful hotel in St. Pete Beach, Florida—the Don Cesar hotel. It looked like a pink castle next to the old wooden hotels on the strip. The following morning, we were blessed with a double rainbow over our hotel. It was like God was smiling down on us. I felt that our Heavenly Father was proud of us and was blessing our marriage. Both our parents were deceased, so having a heavenly affirmation really made our honeymoon special. But what was even more powerful than that rainbow was the realization that I finally broke through after 40 years of waiting—after decades of hurts, frustrations, and disappointments.

Being married was a truly glorious and liberating experience. It was the most glorious experience of my life, in fact. Being married to a man who is tender, kind, loving, generous, extremely patient, incredibly understanding, and a perfect gentleman was more than I had hoped for. In our five years of marriage, Cantrell never once yelled or screamed at me. I used to fear that I might end up with a hot-tempered man. Not so. He is very forgiving when I inadvertently offend or hurt him.

To many, he is so prim and proper—a very serious man

or minister. But behind closed doors, Cantrell is a joker who often makes me laugh until my stomach hurts. We love to laugh at our silly jokes. They say chivalry is dead. I beg to differ. Cantrell opens the car door for me before I get in and before I get out. If I try to open a door myself, he is quick to stop me. Knowing I have a back problem, Cantrell massages my feet and back every night, almost without fail. Some days I feel like I have my private masseur. He regularly prepares breakfast in bed for me on my days off. Or he drives to Starbucks to get me my favorite coffee and pastry. To say that he is generous is an understatement. Since Day One, he has made it his goal to replace my old stuff from Dubai with signature clothes, shoes, and handbags. Today, my closet is bursting at the seams with high-end products and brands that I had never even heard of. And he isn't stopping anytime soon. When we're out and about, he is not shy about carrying my handbag for me.

I often brag about my husband and tell people that he was worth the wait—every millisecond of it. He is not perfect—far from it—but he sure is perfect for me. I know without a shadow of a doubt that he is the best for me. The big and small things that he does for me and the way he loves me almost make me cry sometimes, in a good way. When I was still single, I used to wonder if my future husband would do for me the things that other husbands did for their wives. I was wrong. My husband turned out to be even more thoughtful than many of the married men I had met.

God has truly turned my sorrow into joy. He turned my mourning into dancing. And I believe that is what God wants for you, too. It is my hope and prayer that you, too, will one day meet the best man (or woman) that God has prepared for you. I pray that you will not compromise, no matter how long it takes, or how difficult it gets. The road to your future spouse can seem unending, but you will reach the end eventually. You, too, will see the light at the end of the tunnel. Just don't give up, or you'll never see it. I've always told myself, "If I give up now, I'll be throwing away all the years I have waited." I always encouraged myself, thinking I could wait another day, month, or year. It was hard, I know. But I also knew that I could not afford to give up or compromise. The price was too high to pay. If I gave in, there was no way I could reset or undo what I had done and/or sacrificed.

So, I just kept going; I kept trudging the lonely (for me) path of singleness, hoping and believing for the day I would reach the end. And I did, by God's grace. So never stop trying. Never stop looking, no matter how frustrating it gets. But at the same time, be sure to preserve your heart and soul in the process. Strive to give all of you to your future spouse— not what's left of you. As much as you deserve the best, your spouse also deserves the best version of you. Additionally, I hope that you will be stirred to live your life intentionally for God as you wait for your spouse. Get involved at church, travel the world, and follow your passion. Do not sit around waiting for your future better half. If you do, you will surely regret it later.

Live out your God-given purpose. You are already complete, do not let anyone tell you otherwise. Your future spouse will be a beautiful addition to your life, but you are already complete in Christ with or without him (or her). Never doubt that. Single or not, you already are loved, chosen, cherished, adored, valued, appreciated, prized, gifted, anointed, and celebrated. There is nothing wrong with you, and you are definitely not lacking anything. You are equipped with every spiritual gift to fulfill your call as 1 Corinthians 1:7 promises: "So that ye come behind in no gift; waiting for the coming of our Lord Jesus Christ." You are surely complete and gifted.

It is my fervent prayer that you will find inspiration in our love story. That you, too, will find the love you have been longing for all these years (or decades). Whether you find him (or her) online or offline really doesn't matter. What matters is who you find—a true, godly man (or woman). A person who's not perfect but perfect for you nonetheless. I know that God will remember you just as He remembered us. I believe that one day, you, too, will be able to testify that you found your true love online (or offline). God knows you, sees you, and hears you. He has great plans for you, so take courage. Your true love awaits!

References

Anderson et. al. (2020) Pew Research Center. The Virtues and Downsides of Online Dating. https://www.pewresearch.org/internet/2020/02/06/the-virtues-and-downsides-of-online-dating/#:~:text=Women%20are%20more%20inclined%20than, differing%20attitudes%20about%20the%20topic

Brickfield & Donahue. (2021). What Are the Dangers of Online Dating? https://www.brickdonlaw.com/blog/2021/january/what-are-the-dangers-of-online-dating-/Coates

Coates, Clayton. (2013). Online Dating: Pastor Gives 2 Theories Why Stigma Still Exist. Christian Post. https://www.christianpost.com/news/online-dating-pastor-gives-2-theories-why-stigma-still-exist.html?fbclid=IwAR3BRvQsJSYD6OsITW4T2IcvvkFGj2 92QLtqlp3BDI9-ptqqweT9usIVYwc

EHarmony. (n.d.) Our dating site helps millions find real love. EHarmony. https://www.eharmony.com/

EHarmony. (2021). 10 ONLINE DATING STATISTICS YOU SHOULD KNOW. EHarmony. https://www.eharmony.com/online-dating-statistics/

Harms, William. (2013). Meeting online leads to happier,

more enduring marriages. News Uchicago. https://news.uchicago.edu/story/meeting-online-leads-happier-more-enduring-marriages?fbclid=IwAR13veohEOj7wcnyr6mbaY7tUqT4xgdOOaYOejmaNE8THOb3xHNLm7MoGyA

Heimel & Lamers. (2020). Relationships that Begin Online Less Likely to End in Divorce. https://hllawfirm.com/2013/07/18/relationships-online-divorce/

ICE. (2022). Dating or Defrauding? PROTECT YOUR-SELF AGAINST ROMANCE SCAMS. U.S. Immigration and Customs Enforcement. https://www.ice.gov/features/romance-scams#:~:text=Total%20reported%20losses%20to%20romance,it%20was%20five%20years%20prior

Increditools. (2023). How Many Couples Meet Online in 2023? (Quick Stats). Increditools. https://increditools.com/how-many-couples-meet-online/

Lazic, Marija. (2022). 41 Shocking Scam Statistics to Keep You Safe in 2022. Legaljobs. https://legaljobs.io/blog/scam-statistics/

Lefroy, Emily. (2022). Sexual predators use dating apps to hunt for vulnerable victims: study. New York Post. https://nypost.com/2022/11/28/sexual-predators-use-dating-apps-to-hunt-for-victims-study/

OUTVoices. (2022). New to online dating? Here's how to protect yourself. OUTVoices. https://outvoices.us/online-dating-safety-tips

Palmer, Scott & Bethany. (2022). 5 Reasons Why Money Is The #1 Cause of Divorce. Crosswalk. https://www.crosswalk.com/family/finances/5-reasons-why-money-is-the-1-cause-of-divorce.html

Patteson, Callie. (2020) Dating app denial: For some couples, the stigma of meeting online still holds. Today. https://www.today.com/tmrw/dating-app-denial-some-couples-stigma-meeting-online-still-holds-t173081?fbclid=IwAR0LlTNpHHZI18BoIZ6rRIQowjgfbxt-Z3IU7HPkPCNgWkNOrcHfObqvnWA

Piper, John. (2009). Questions to Ask When Preparing for Marriage. Desiring God. https://www.desiringgod.org/articles/questions-to-ask-when-preparing-for-marriage

Piper, John. (2014). Is Online Dating Good for Christians? Desiring God. https://www.desiringgod.org/interviews/is-online-dating-good-for-christians

Vuleta, Branka. (2022). 14 Divorce Statistics You Need to Know in 2022. Legaljobs. https://legaljobs.io/blog/divorce-statistics/

Acknowledgment

Thank you to Ms. Karen Bradford for proofreading my manuscript.

Maricel Colquit currently lives with her husband in Dallas, TX. She considers faith and family the most important in her life. She hopes her works will inspire and equip single women (and men) to live intentionally while waiting for their spouse. When not writing or vlogging, Maricel loves to read, watch movies, go to the Opera, and tend her mini rose garden. Visit www.maricelcolquit.com to learn more.

www.ingramcontent.com/pod-product-compliance
Lightning Source LLC
Chambersburg PA
CBHW032057020426

42335CB00011B/381